Joe Dew
A Glorious Life

By Elaine Briggs

With much love this book is dedicated to
My father and mother

Joseph and Evelyn Dew

TABLE OF CONTENTS

APPENDICES 199

Acknowledgements

Thanks to so many for their help and support in writing this book.

Many thanks to Hazel Whitney, my father's classmate beginning in grade school. She shared stories about my dad, news articles from WWII, school play fliers, photos, and a copy of the *Quasquicentennial, Redfield, Iowa, 1860-1985*, by Margaret Morrison. Thanks also to classmates Lavern Sloan and Beulah Dicky for their stories.

My mother had written a brief story of her life before she died that helped fill in a lot of details. Aunt Goldie's saved boxes of pictures and scraps of papers with bits of information were invaluable. I so appreciate my brother, Dennis, who had heard the stories long before I had and explained some of the mechanical things I didn't understand. You died too young, my dear brother. Dennis' son, Joshua Dew, read and commented on parts of the book.

Thanks to my Dew cousins. Mary Streeter, John Dew's daughter, shared dates and information about her father's World War II service. LaVon Dew Asher and her sister Robin Dew Love helped with names, dates, information, and pictures of their grandfather John Dew and their father Harold Leroy Dew. Julie Kitterman, DeElda Dew's granddaughter, shared info and pictures. Jack Pruett shared information about his mother Arlene Dew and the Dew's ancestry leading back to Charlemagne from a reverse ancestry done by attorneys on a small inheritance after Edna Dew had passed.

Thanks to Hazel Glaspel Johnson, wife of my mom's brother Carl, for the work she passed on about the Johnson family history. Thanks to my Johnson cousins. Gwen Johnston Day supplied information about my mom's favorite brother Willis Johnston. Carla Hillgren, Ola Johnson's granddaughter, did an extensive Johnson/Johnston family tree and sent pictures. Kathy Lehr, Clarence Johnston's daughter, kindly shared pictures and family information.

Thanks to Becky S. Jordan, reference specialist for Special Collections in the University Archives of Iowa State University for sending me information about the college and copies of the college catalog from 1937 and 1938.

My understanding of my dad's war years would not have been possible without the internet. Dave Wiltrout's website taxyman.com (no longer on the web) led me to the 741st Company C's booklet, *Vitamin Charley*, written by Smith, Meacham, and Hillner, which was shared by the son of SSG Ernest O. Padgett. Thank you Command Sergeant Major (Retired) Joseph E. Padgett for your information and kind words. Robert E. Passanisi, Merrill's Marauders Association Historian, provided a timeline for John Dew's service during World War II in the 475th Infantry Regiment.

Thanks to Dr. Sarah Garfinkel, Research Fellow in Emotion and Neuroscience at Brighton and Sussex Medical School, Sussex University, England, investigating the mechanisms underlying learning and memory, for the insights you shared with me on memory.

Thank you Aurélie Pilet for the information about Chillon Castle in Switzerland via email. We were most fortunate to get you for our tour guide when we visited.

Many thanks to Jeanne and John Meszaros, Sue Hass, and Carol Phelps for their suggestions and input, and to all friends who encouraged me along the way. Special thanks to my friend Sandi Freburger for your enthusiasm and encouragement.

Thanks to FreshStartWriting.com-Adrienne Hovey who skillfully and gently edited my book.

Thanks to James Schapiro for your writing insights and pictures of Trinity Church on Wall Street and Radio City Music Hall in New York City.

Thanks to Bill Warnock who answered many questions. Your extensive knowledge is amazing. Good luck with your book *741st Tank Battalion in World War II D-Day to VE-Day* and your website, *etohistory.com*. I'm excited to read your book when it comes out.

Thanks to my friend Pat Bernier for your wizardry in restoring several of my dad's old pictures. The restoration is pure magic.

Special thanks to Nihal Riad, English teacher, librarian, and friend, who kindly provided critical feedback and encouragement after reading my entire book multiple times. It would have been difficult to write this book without you and all your expert help.

My grandchildren's help and enthusiasm spurred me on. Thanks to Keith, Kyle, Emily, and Michael Briggs and Cherokee, Cheyenne, and Christian Gonzalez. Keith you saved me more than once with your knowledge of computers and programs, especially how to use Gimp. Emily, who knew making a table of contents and numbering pages could be such a challenge! You are awesome!

Thank you to my son Brian for your patient help with all things computers, and to my son Jeff and his wife Brandie for pictures of Mosquito Creek and family tombstones when you stopped in Iowa. Thanks to Brandie for sharing your patient's memoir. It gave me the idea of including my mom's stories and makes my book feel complete.

And special thanks to my patient and loving husband who supported and helped me in caring for my father and throughout my journey of writing of his story.

Preface

My father was an amazing man, but I had never gotten to know him like I knew my mom. My mom and I were the ones who talked on the phone and sat and visited whenever we all got together. My mother was my best friend and she loved me unconditionally. I knew how she felt about everything. I knew my father loved me and I loved him, but I didn't *know* him. When my mom died at the young age of 68, I felt a deep, deep loss. My mother had been my father's world and he was lost too.

The journey to get to know my dad truly began after my mother died. A couple of times each month I made the hour and a half drive to visit my dad in Flint, Michigan. Our activity rarely varied: out to lunch at Country Buffet, where we met with a group of seniors affectionately known as the lunch bunch, and then home to his apartment where I asked him to tell me his life stories, and I wrote them down.

I always knew my father was very intelligent, but the specifics of his life he could remember truly amazed me. The number of detailed stories he shared with me going back to age four and his childhood was astonishing. I learned that not only did he have a high IQ, but a keen episodic memory as well. I filled yellow pad after yellow pad with his anecdotes.

Over the years, I had a stack of pads more than a foot high with stories about his growing up as the son of a blacksmith in rural Iowa during the Depression, his experiences riding the rails to find work in the West, traveling to Kodiak, Alaska to work on building the naval base there, fighting in World War II with the 741st Tank Battalion, and moving to Michigan after graduating from college to work for General Motors.

Starting out, writing down his stories was a way to have something to do when I visited my dad. But that changed. When he asked me what I was going to do with all those stories, I smiled, hugged him, and told him I was going to write a book about the amazing life of Joe Dew. We laughed, but I knew he was touched. He softly said, "It has been a glorious life."

Well, my dear dad, I fulfilled my promise. Writing this book has been a challenging journey and I could not be more pleased that your story is at last written.

I love you, Dad. What a gift it is to have your life stories and be able to share them! I've kept them as close to your words as possible. I am so very grateful for our time together.

Family of Joseph Harold Dew

Grandparents

 AND

John T. Dew   AND   Mary (Molly) Jane Auld
3-11-1842 to 3-15-1902   11-30-1841 to 11-25-1927

Parents

 AND

Joseph Locke Dew   AND   Edna May Berg
9-13-1879 to 10-5-1946   8-20-1887 to 1-8-1947

Dew Siblings

Goldie	Echo	John	DeElda
1-26-1908	8-13-1909	1-18-1912	6-19-1914
2-26-1986	11-28-1992	11-27-1972	5-23-1940

Arlene	Joe	Jim
3-15-1917	1-1-1920	3-18-1930
10-27-1965	7-9-2003	3-01-1975

Memories of Growing Up Poor

Joe and Spot

The Beginning

New Year's Day, 1920, Edna Dew lay spent on the bed, relieved her sixth child, Joseph Harold Dew, had made it into the cold wintry Iowa world safely. No one was by the bed to help except her twelve-year-old eldest daughter, Goldie. Little Joe was wrapped in a blanket on her chest, sleeping and breathing softly.

Edna heaved a sigh and closed her eyes. What future would this child have? Truth be told, Edna hadn't really wanted this little Joe. Money was tight. Times were tough, although, they hadn't always been. When she'd married handsome, blue-eyed, blond-haired, strong Joseph, Edna had thought her life was finally on the right track.

Edna wished her mother could have been with her, but she had died when Edna was only twelve years old. She had been by her mother's side through all the horrible weeks, as she suffered a slow and painful death from Bright's disease. She treasured a small, pink Cupid dish her mother had given her that had been in the family since the 1800s. It was the only keepsake Edna had of her mother and she missed her horribly.

Edna age 8

Cupid dish

Then at age sixteen, Edna married a much older man, a neighboring farmer by the name of Austey. The union did not go well. Barely six months after her marriage, Edna's father picked her up with the wagon and took her home. Shortly thereafter, her father filed the appropriate papers and her marriage was annulled.

In the small rural Illinois town, everyone knew everyone's business. The stigma and humiliation of the annulment spurred Edna's father to arrange for her to travel to Des Moines, Iowa, nearly 500 miles away, far from her home and far from her family in Mt. Erie, Illinois. There she worked as a domestic in the home of family friends, the Critchett family, well-to-do owners of the Critchett Piano and Organ Company.

But as she lay in bed with her baby by her side that cold January morning, Edna's thoughts drifted to her husband, Joseph Locke Dew. She had met Joseph in Des Moines. Joseph was different. He had a trade. He was a blacksmith. He was good-looking with powerful muscles, a ready laugh, and joking manner. Eight years older than Edna, Joseph was settled. She believed he was going somewhere. She was in love and knew this time her life would be good.

Nineteen-year-old Edna was sure Joseph was the right man and this was the life she wanted. After meeting in March, they were married April 20, 1907, in Des Moines, ready to start a good life in Gilmore City, Iowa. Edna fondly remembered their first home: a comfortable white house with a proper parlor, right in town. As an apprentice, Joseph had worked hard and learned blacksmithing. Joseph then bought his own business and was making very good money, nearly $40 per week. They had money, a good life, and the start of a beautiful family.

1910 Edna, Joseph, Goldie, Echo | **1912 Goldie, John, Echo**

As she lay on the bed with baby Joe by her side, she remembered the blacksmith shops Joseph had had in Gilmore City, Stout, then Berlin, then back to Gilmore City, then Corwith. They had stayed two years in Grand Junction and two years in Glidden. And now they were living in Tracey. Joseph was skillful at buying a struggling business, building it up, and then selling it for a profit. But so many moves!

Joseph Locke Dew
Third from left

4

The J.L. Dew Blacksmith Shop had a good reputation for quality craftsmanship and Joseph was a hard worker. He was mechanical, good with numbers, and affable. But by the time little Joe was born, his business was struggling. His skills at making tools for the home like spatulas, cooking utensils, knives, farm sickles, hammers, axes, and even simple items like nails were being replaced by machines that more quickly and cheaply mass-produced the items. The need for horseshoeing and wagon wheels was being displaced by innovations in manufactured automobiles and farm equipment. No longer did every home and business depend on the skills of a local blacksmith.

Thirteen years after their marriage, they were in Tracy, Iowa to start yet another blacksmith shop. In order to offset the slowdown in business, Joseph had reluctantly taken a job at a nearby cement plant to meet the expenses of his growing family. Joseph hated working at the cement plant. He hated coming home covered in grime from head to toe, breathing in and coughing out the foul, gritty dust. Most especially, he hated having a boss tell him what to do. Joseph was frustrated with his life.

October 25, 1919, a dark and windy night, Joseph left the blacksmith shop to deliver sharpened plow lays to a farmer a mile out of town and didn't arrive back home in time for dinner. Pacing and frantic with worry, pregnant Edna finally woke Goldie at midnight and sent her to Dr. Park's to use the phone. "Dr. Park called Farmer Cavern," a sleepy Goldie told her mother. "He told the doctor that dad left by eight o'clock." There was no doubt in Edna's mind when she heard the news.

As the crisp morning light crept in, Joseph opened the door into the kitchen. Edna was waiting. Her eyes flashed as she grabbed the nearest wooden chair and smashed it over his head. She turned on her heel and slammed the door to their bedroom. She had never been so mad in her entire life. Joseph had spent the night out drinking and gambling. From then on, cards were banned from the home.

On Monday morning when Goldie walked into class at school, cold stares greeted her. "Goldie's dad is an expert poker player," classmate Dwight Hogate ranted to everyone. "He skinned my father out of all his money!" The scandal reached the teacher's ears and Goldie's job as treasurer for the sixth-grade class was taken from her and given to Lottie Dunsmore. Goldie was mortified. According to Goldie, finishing sixth grade was almost unbearable.

However, Goldie's one great joy during her sixth-grade year was when she held little Joe at her mother's bedside on that cold New Year's morning. She had felt so blissfully happy. She felt a bond and a love that would last all her life.

"Goldie, you need to stay home from school this week and look after things," her father pronounced. Echo, John, and DeElda went off to school, while Goldie stayed home and did the housework and cooking. While Mother stayed in bed and recuperated, Goldie looked after three-year-old Arlene and baby Joe. A neighbor, Mrs. Frye, looked in every morning to check on mother and baby. When Goldie finally returned to school, her teacher wanted an excuse from her parents explaining her absence. Her dad flatly refused to write her one. "Everyone in town knows there is a new baby at our house," he snapped.

Without an excuse, Goldie's teacher made her stay in every day during recess. On Friday afternoon, Goldie's teacher marched her upstairs to the principal's office. "There are 400 pupils in this school, Goldie," admonished the principal, "and each and every one has to bring in a written excuse when they are absent. You are no exception!"

At home, her dad wouldn't yield an inch. According to Goldie, "Talking to him was like trying to talk to a stone wall. I thought I was ready to burst." Monday morning came and Goldie adamantly refused to go to school without an excuse. Finally, Mother relented, gave Goldie a stern look, and a warning not to tell her dad. Goldie tucked the note in her pocket, bent to kiss baby Joe's head, and tromped off to school with her pigtails flapping.

Months passed, and after a cold, blustery winter came the renewal of spring. Life gradually settled into a normal rhythm. Joseph working. Edna taking care of the home. Goldie, Echo, John, and DeElda going to school. Three-year-old Arlene and baby Joe demanding a great deal of attention.

The Move to Redfield, Iowa

Several years after Joe was born, Joseph saw an ad in the paper for a blacksmith shop in the little town of Redfield, more than 80 miles west of Tracey. It sounded promising, so Joseph made the long trip to look things over. He soon cut a deal with the owner and once again had a shop he hoped he could build up and make a living for his family. He moved his tools and set up shop. According to Joe's classmate, Hazel Whitney, "I remember the blacksmith shop on Main Street in between the grocer's store and the doctor's office." Joseph started the business and stayed until March with occasional trips back to Tracey. Then in early spring, he moved his family to their new home.

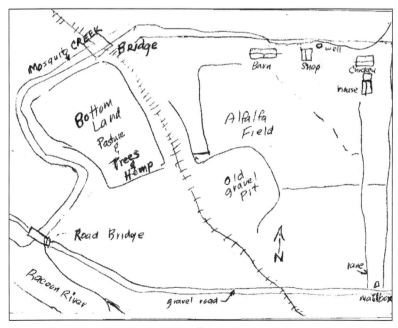

Edna had always been afraid of Indians and was a little wary when she first saw the rutted, winding lane leading to the house, hidden in a stand of trees, about a quarter of a mile back from the road. The hilly homestead along the railroad tracks was small with fields all around. Only four of the nine and a half acres were tillable. It felt isolated and lonely. Despite her many misgivings, Edna vehemently declared to her husband, "Joseph, we are staying here forever!"

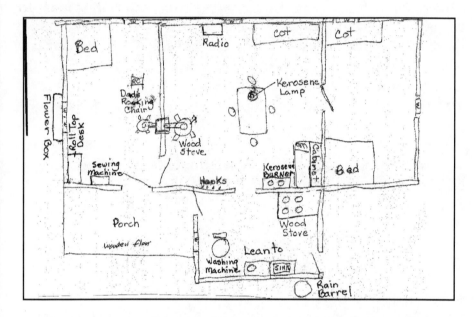

Edna was determined to make this a home for her family. Using the tightly woven, colorful print cloth saved from sturdy 50-pound flour sacks and her Singer treadle sewing machine, she brightened the inside of the sparsely furnished rooms with curtains and quilts. Thrifty Edna knew how to stretch what little money they had.

Joseph, ever handy, expanded the home with lean-tos for the cook stove and another bedroom. There were 2 bedrooms for the family of 8: parents in one room, girls in another, and boys on cots in the kitchen. Even with their tiffs, there was a lot of love shown by the daily deeds Joseph did for his wife in their new home.

By necessity, Edna never spent much money, but she did send away for seed from the popular Henry Field Seed Company in Shenandoah, Iowa. Their slogan was *Seeds that Yield are Sold by Field.* In addition to her large garden, she grew striking orange tiger lilies, intense red poppies, deep purple irises, and brilliant pink peonies. Clumps of fragrant lavender and deep purple lilacs dotted the yard. Bouquets of wildflowers cheered the table: violets, Dutchmen's britches, and bluebells. Tall, stately, red, white, and pink hollyhocks provided the girls with big, colorful blooms to make dolls all summer long.

DeElda and hollyhocks

Rhode Island Reds, scratching in the yard and throwing up puffs of dust, were Edna's pride and joy. Joseph made nests for the chicken coop out of thin wooden crates scavenged from the town grocer. Everything, but everything, was saved and put to good use.

Every week, whatever eggs the family didn't eat were crated up on Saturday. Little Joe sat next to his dad and rode to town to sell the beautiful brown eggs for 10 cents a dozen at A.J. Woods' store in Redfield. One snowy winter day, Joe's dad missed a curve and ended up in the ditch with over half the eggs dripping messily from the crate. Dad shook his finger at little Joe and threatened him, "Don't you dare tell your mother what happened to her eggs." Edna got her egg money as usual, none the wiser.

As Joe recalled, his dad joked a lot and teased his mother unmercifully. "There are the high Dutch, and the low Dutch; but Edna, you're part of the damned Dutch." Edna, with her hazel blue-green eyes blazing, threw the Sears Roebuck catalog at him. But that wasn't the end of his teasing. Passing gas was embarrassing enough, but Joseph teased Edna with a singsong refrain, "Toot of a toot of a toot la toot." Mother abhorred being made fun of, but Joseph would grab her around the waist and try to kiss away her protests and chided:

"Oh, how sweet, but oh how bitter,
To kiss an old tobacco spitter."

DeElda and Arlene

Saturday nights found the Dew home graced with music. Joe's grandfather John T. Dew, a Civil War veteran, had taught Joe's father how to play the violin. Joe's older sister, Arlene, took lessons on the violin and played at school. Sweet-tempered DeElda enjoyed playing along with the accordion. Edna, with her waist-length

10

brown hair wrapped tightly in a bun, played the harmonica. They even had a small Hawaiian guitar Joseph let Joe strum when he was little. The family truly enjoyed being together and playing music.

When Edna felt melancholy, she sang her favorite song, *"Hello Central,"* a hit published in 1901 and that reminded her of her mother. About a little girl trying to telephone her mother in heaven, the song tugged on the public's heartstrings and sold nearly a million copies.

HELLO CENTRAL, GIVE ME HEAVEN
Charles K. Harris

Papa I'm so sad and lonely
Sobbed a tearful little child.
Since dear Mama's gone to heaven
Papa darling, you've not smiled.
I will speak to her and tell her
That we want her to come home.
Just you listen and I'll call her
Through the telephone.

Hello Central, give me heaven
For my Mama's there
You can find her with the angels
On the golden stair.
She'll be glad it's me who's speaking
Call her won't you please
For I want to surely tell her
We're so lonely here.

When the girl received this message
Coming o'er the telephone
How her heart thrilled in that moment
And the wires seemed to moan
I will answer just to please her
"Yes, dear heart, I'll soon come home."
Kiss me Mama, kiss your darling
Through the telephone.

As well as being a house filled with music, Edna wanted her children to get a good education, even though she had only gone to the fifth grade. She believed strongly in the value of an education and pushed all of her children to graduate from high school. Although Joseph had only gone to the third grade, he also valued education. He was especially good with mathematics and that helped him in his business. Both Edna and Joseph wanted their children to have a better life than they had and they believed an education would make a difference.

Joseph loved to tell the story of a blacksmith he knew who hadn't been so good with numbers. The blacksmith used the whitewashed wall of his shop to write down the accounts of the people owing him money. One day, a kid helping him whitewashed over all the accounts. What a disaster! And what laughs Joseph got when he told the story!

The J.L. Dew Blacksmith Shop

Joseph was optimistic about his new shop in Redfield. He got it organized and hung up his sign. He enjoyed being his own boss and working with his hands. No more cement factory work for him. He horseshoed mules, riding horses, and draft horses used for pulling heavy loads. Sometimes a big mule train would stop at his blacksmith shop and he would be busy pounding on new horseshoes all day. He also worked on pug mill knives for the brickyard mixing equipment at the Redfield Bridge & Tile Works.

He made all sorts of items for the home, sharpening skates in the winter, and making any kitchen utensils needed, such as water ladles for the homemakers of Redfield and the neighboring towns and countryside. The bulk of his business, however, was the making and sharpening of farm tools and shoeing horses.

Spatula made by Joseph

The heavy plow lays he made were "pointed" by fusing on a new tip using the roaring heat in the forge, shaping the pieces together on the anvil with heavy hammer blows, quenching in the tub, and grinding on emery wheels to sharpen and take out the nicks and flaws from the trip hammer. Polishing wheels were used to give a mirror finish so the plow lays scoured cleanly through the turned earth. Cultivator shovels were painstakingly shaped, sharpened, and polished. Disk blades were finely sharpened so they could cut through cornstalks and stubble. Inventive Joseph developed his own technique to sharpen disk blades without disassembling them, saving lots of time and effort.

According to Joe, "My father was a master at judging the best metal to use, the heat of the forge, and picking just the right quenching solution. He jealously guarded his quenching formula for the slack tub where he cooled the metal. The quenching formula made a big difference in the strength of the steel and its ability to be springy or hardened."

Come fall, many wagons stopped at his blacksmith shop to have the loosened steel bands shrunk on the wooden wheels. Joseph removed each old band and shrank the circumference by heating the band cherry red to expand it, then replaced it, and quenched it in the tub. The quenched wheels crackled and popped as the metal tires tightened on the wooden frames. The rate of cooling was extremely important. Joseph prided himself on his skills to forge-weld broken buggy springs and have just the right spring. Few blacksmiths were as skillful.

A big forge, steamy hot in the summer and with welcome warmth in the winter, the J.L. Dew Blacksmith Shop was a meeting place for the men of the community who would stop by to joke with Joseph, talk politics, gossip, or play a game of washers out back under the shade of the trees along the alley. Joseph was liked by all.

Joseph standing by anvil

Standing six feet tall, large arms and a barrel chest, blue twinkling eyes, blond hair, and a ready laugh and joking manner, Joseph occasionally made an extra 25 cents betting he could pick up the 150-pound anvil one-armed. It was an easy trick for him as he wrapped his belt around the anvil's horn. With the use of the leather belt and muscles hardened by years of hard work, Joe's dad easily lifted the anvil in one fell swoop. Little Joe marveled at his father's strength when he saw him pick up two anvils and slam them together with a loud clang and no resulting rebound.

On one occasion, a young woman came into the blacksmith shop, needing the tire on her Model T changed. Joseph stuck the crank in the front, lifted the whole car, and had little Joe stick a block underneath to hold up the car. No small accomplishment to lift over 1,500 pounds. Another time, he helped an old lady whose car stalled going uphill. Joseph grabbed the front end of the car, lifted it, and walked it around so it faced downhill. With a push, he jumped in, popped the clutch, and the car readily started.

Little Joe spent many hours playing in his father's shop. Pounding nails into the dirt out back. Watching the comings and goings of the road gangs and their long lines of mules. Hearing the loud clang of the hammer as his father nailed on one shoe after another. Listening as his father bantered with the men or carried on a serious horse trade.

Joe remembered watching as a battered junk wagon lumbered to a stop in front of the blacksmith shop, its rusty tin bells clanging its arrival. A monthly visitor to the shop, the bearded Jewish peddler in his long black coat climbed down from the wagon. He and his helper, a burly black man, traveled from Des Moines to buy junk and sell whatever they could. They were always eager to make their first deal of the day at the blacksmith shop, which they believed foretold their luck for the entire day. They looked over the scrap materials Joseph had and set about dickering. Whether it was 30 cents a pound for copper in the radiators, an aluminum starter, or $4 for a 300-pound cast-iron engine, Joseph always got a good deal. Learning the knack of making a deal from his father was truly a skill that served Joe well throughout his life.

Joe's dad had many skills and even brought home watches and clocks to repair. Joe would watch in fascination as his father sat at the table in the glow of the kerosene lamp, disassembling a watch with all its tiny parts and even tinier springs. The 2" by 1.5" vise and the small jeweler's hammer didn't seem as if they could even fit in his father's big hands. But he always got the job done, no matter how intricate the work.

Childhood Memories

Although the family struggled to survive through the Depression and with the added onus of the decline of blacksmithing due to the Industrial Revolution, Joe's childhood was filled with plenty of fun and adventures making him strong and self-reliant. After dinner, little Joe always hiked to the end of the lane to get the Des Moines Tribune. It cost three cents a day, but it was an appreciated luxury. He climbed up on his dad's lap in the old rocking chair while his dad adjusted the small piece of cardboard in the arm of his glasses to keep the light from the kerosene lamp from shining in his eyes.

Then his dad read the funnies to little Joe, whose favorite comic strip was Ben Webster and his dog, Briar. Ben and Briar rescued damsels in distress and faced crooked bank executives, who manipulated mortgages so they could steal the homes of hard-working, honest people. The comic strip was chock full of adventure and lots of fun for Joe, as well as the enjoyment of spending time with his father.

Joe flourished in the hilly, Iowa countryside. With five older siblings, he was often left to his own devices. A number of times, Joe got into fixes and had to be rescued. As a storm brewed, Joe climbed onto a branch hanging over the rushing waters of the Raccoon River in the spring and couldn't get down. According to him, his calls for help were finally heard by his mother. Unfazed, she simply hollered at his dad, "Sounds like Joe's in trouble. Go get him."

On another occasion, little Joe was helping his father burn brush. The fire was going really well, because Joe had just dumped on some kerosene. He still had the kerosene can in his hand when he heard his father frantically yell, "Throw it! Throw it!" Joe threw it and the next instant, the can exploded in mid-air. When the flaming can landed, the entire pasture caught on fire and burned down. His father was upset, but relieved Joe wasn't hurt. According to Joe, "My dad always took things in stride and wasn't easily flustered."

Another day in the sheep pasture just east of the house, Joe was knocked down several times and finally cornered by the neighbor's ram whose curved horns were looking mighty dangerous. Joe's yells for help were finally heard by his mother, who came running with the pitchfork to get him out of this truly perilous predicament.

Joe had fond memories of his times with his siblings. He remembered he and his older brother John were steady companions. When Joe was just a blond-haired tyke, John sent him fishing in a small creek on the north side of the house. Joe shouldered his homemade fishing pole made from a branch with a string from the store-wrapped bread and a bent pin for his hook and happily marched over to the creek. In summer, the creek dried up and the minnows were easy pickings. Then John sent Joe back to the house on an errand while he caught a big carp and put it on Joe's little fishing pole. Joe was overjoyed when he saw the huge carp "he" had caught. Joe and John always had a good time and found something to entertain themselves.

Joe and John also worked hard together, but the work was often lightened by good, clean fun. John delighted in playing tricks on his younger brother. He knew when cows ate green leaves, they got loose as a goose. Feeling particularly mischievous, he covered a huge cow pie with leaves and sand. He told Joe he would give him a nickel if he'd dig down to the mud. A nickel was a lot in those days, so Joe excitedly dove in with both hands. However, tears started flowing when he realized what he had gotten into. John

17

took pity on him and walked him down to the creek to wash off the slimy, smelly cow dung.

Joe's sister Arlene, who was three years older, had real spirit and often got into mischief with her shenanigans. One sunshiny summer day, she pulled DeElda in the wagon down the lane with little Joe pushing. She started running as fast as her feet would carry her, turned the corner really fast, dumped screaming DeElda out, and caused Joe to smash head first into the ground. An older Arlene got mad at Joe when he corrected her after she said the car had a VH engine. "Arlene," gibed Joe, "it's not VH, it's V8." Furious at being corrected, Arlene picked up a brick and hurled it at Joe, hitting his front tooth and knocking a chip out of it.

On an adventure at the age of six, Joe wandered off to go fishing for goldfish, but didn't tell his mother. The pond was alongside the railroad tracks three-quarters of the way to town. Joe's folks had been looking for him for some time when he returned home just as the sun was going down. Joe knew he was in trouble when he spied his dad halfway up the lane. "Boy, when you go by me you better be moving!" growled his father. Joe recalled, "I didn't feel a thing as I flew by my dad who was swinging a long hickory switch."

Joe's mother dearly loved her cats, whether on her lap or curled up in the corner. She always kept one in the house to keep it free of mice. Mouser was her favorite, smoky gray and fat. Joe, on the other hand, absolutely hated that cat. When he walked into the lean-to kitchen with two buckets full of well water, there sat Mouser. Joe let out a deep growl. Startled, Mouser sprang up and broke the window trying to get out of Joe's way. His mother's wagging finger and stern words put Joe in his place. Luckily, the cat was fine, but the window had to be fixed.

Joe frequently went west of the house where there was a gravel pit left by the railroad crew when they constructed the track. After hauling out the gravel, what remained was a deep pit with no water in it. It was a good spot for finding grubs for fishing. There also were a number of six-foot-long railroad ties that had been left behind. Joe and his friends used them to construct a hideout, sawing and piecing the ties together. They made a roof from sod and gravel and fashioned a door out of discarded wood. Quite the place to sit and think or play cowboys and Indians with his friends. And, oh, the fun of building something.

On Mosquito Creek north of the homestead by the big hill, there had been a small Indian village. During the summers, Joe searched the dry creek beds for Indian artifacts. Every once in a while, he found arrowheads. His dad had some sharp-pointed arrowheads he told Joe were dipped in poison to bring down game. Joe also found a heavy tomahawk and marveled at the craftsmanship to create such tools from stone.

Arrowheads

Axe head

Joe remembered when the tooth fairy was a visitor to the Dew home, bringing some small special treat, but never money. Christmas was the most special holiday of the year. Joe and his father went into the snowy woods, cut down a tree, and hauled it home. The girls happily chattered together while they all made decorations and used the tin foil from old Ford condenser coils to cut out shiny ornaments. Although no candles were ever put on the tree, the family being ever conscious of expenses, it still looked beautiful when completely decorated. One present was all the children ever got, usually something practical. A special surprise Joe got one year and fondly remembered was a little toy Santa Claus he played with for hours. Christmas was a very exciting and memorable holiday for the children of the Dew household.

Summertime

With the coming of summer, shoes were put away to save for the fall and the children went barefoot. Joe's feet were so callused he could walk on the hot, steel rails of the nearby railroad track and even on the jagged cinders. A field of alfalfa stubble was another story. As Joe recalled, "I had to run across it if I didn't want my feet punctured by the hard, dried spikes."

Summertime also meant fishing. Joe fashioned a slingshot out of discarded rubber inner tubes, practicing and practicing his shooting. Finally, from six feet away, he could take out a whole slew of grasshoppers. The short, fat, yellow grasshopper bodies were the best bait for catching fish. Joe figured out the darker grasshoppers weren't as good for fishing, because they had longer wings and not as juicy bodies.

One time while fishing, Joe ended up with a scar he carried for the rest of his life. As Joe threw out the line, a hook burrowed deep into the meaty part of his hand, just below his thumb. He cut the line and made his way home. Not being able to get the hook out, his mother sent him walking to the doctor in Redfield, a mile away by the railroad tracks. When he arrived, Dr. Moorman picked up his scalpel and dug deep to carve out the firmly attached hook. Then the doctor dabbed the wound with iodine, bandaged him up, and asked if he wanted the hook. Ever thrifty, Joe, of course, said yes and made the mile walk home with a throbbing hand.

While Joe was growing up during the Depression, there were years of record heat and drought in Iowa. The Iowa summers were so hot sweat beaded on Joe's forehead even when he sat in the shade. The hottest day on record was July 20, 1934, when it hit 118 degrees. Dips in the river were a grand way to cool off. Lester Chambers, the neighbor boy, and Joe had a special swimming hole. Unfortunately, this big ol' water moccasin liked it too. The boys had to keep an eye on it as the long, heavy snake lay coiled on the bank sunning itself. The water moccasins along with the occasional snapping turtle added a daring thrill to the cooling summertime dips.

To keep cool on those especially hot, muggy summer nights, Joe and his older brother John wet newspapers with cold water from the well and put them on the linoleum floor, sleeping on them in only their underpants. In the winter, it was a different story. On cold nights, bricks were heated, wrapped in newspapers, and put under the covers to ward off the cold. No electricity, no fans, no insulation, and over 100-degree temperatures in the summer and well below zero degrees in the snowy, blustery winter. It was a tough life.

An infrequent hailstorm in the steamy summer meant the opportunity for a real treat: ice cream. As hail pounded down, it was quickly scooped into a metal container where the thick, rich cream from Betsy the cow was cranked and turned into a lip-smacking, delicious treat.

The Fourth of July was always a memorable holiday. The family sat on blankets out on the front lawn after dark to enjoy the show. Joe's dad brought home cheap fireworks from town he got for a penny apiece. He carefully tied several together and lit one. As soon as the match touched the fuse, they could hear the sizzle and all waited in anticipation for the exciting display. Dad threw the bunch high into the night sky. Flitting fireflies and sparkling fireworks. What a display!

Dad always bought one huge 18-inch rocket firecracker for the final event. He taped the end onto the launcher he had made out of angle iron and aimed it toward the railroad tracks. The massive firecracker slid along the tilted, 8-foot-long angle iron before vaulting high into the sky. The family watched with wonder at the beautiful cascades. "That was a real thrill!" reminisced Joe.

Everyone in Joe's family looked forward to the Old Settlers Reunion, a summer tradition started in Redfield in 1887. All the families in the community and neighboring farms came together, young and old, and brought a family picnic to Hanging Rock along the picturesque Raccoon River. Sporting events were the highlight,

21

with prizes donated by the Redfield merchants and those of the neighboring towns. Band concerts and vocal music, as well as political speeches and talks by old settlers, filled the day. Carnival time for the children with rides and treats was popular. The merry-go-round cost 5 cents and a ride on the Ferris wheel was 10 cents. It was a special time to get together and meet with scattered families and old-time friends.

As the festive parade was about to start, Joe was so excited. Ever looking to make some money, he was happy to be offered 10 cents to carry a sign on his back. Proudly lining up to walk in the parade, his father spied him and yelled, "You take that back to where you got it and give the man his sign." No 10 cents for him that day.

Old Settler's Parade   **Hanging Rock**

Another summer activity was the Dew family reunion held at Aunt Winnie and Uncle Charley's home. Aunts and uncles and lots of cousins running around and having fun. Everyone bringing something to eat. It was a day Joe never went hungry. Among the whispered talk was a secret old Grandma Auld, who had gone blind from cataracts, told Joe's older sister Goldie: "We are related to Mary, Queen of Scots, but don't you dare tell anybody. It was scandalous. Mary was beheaded!"

Dew Reunion 1916

Chores and More Chores

Chores were a part of everyday survival for everyone in the family. Hard work started for Joe at an early age. He was given lots of responsibility and expected to do his share helping around the homestead. The lane to the house from the gravel road was narrow and rutted. Joe's job was to fill the ruts, even though his dad continually made more. From early childhood, Joe carried the wood for the stove and stacked it on the kitchen floor. Another job little Joe had to do, and hated, was taking the chamber pot to the outhouse to dump.

The bottomland on the homestead had cottonwood and elm trees which were good for fence posts. When Joe was small, he would pile the brush as the trees were cut. As he got older, he would be on his knees pulling the 7-foot–long crosscut saw with his older brother John. When older yet, Joe cut the trees into long logs by himself. Then his father hired a neighbor with a double team of horses to come over and the long logs were dragged to the yard.

After the logs dried out, another neighbor came with a buzz saw to cut the logs into stove-length pieces to be split and used in the cook stove. Joe's dad cautioned him to be very careful around the mechanical saw as he himself had lost his index finger when using a buzz saw as a young boy. To finish the chore, Joe used the axe to split then stack the wood for the family to use. Years later, they got a kerosene stove with an oven sitting on the top. Joe had to fill it with the smelly kerosene and was warned by his mother not to spill a drop.

Joe worked side by side with his dad and older brother to cut down trees to improve the pasture for the cows. At noontime, Mother walked to the pasture with fried egg sandwiches and they sat under the shade of a tree while resting and eating their lunch with the birds singing above them.

Joe often stopped at the bottom of the hill to get a drink of water out of the long-handled dipper before he carried water from the well up the hill in three-gallon bucketfuls, two at a time. To save some of the need for lugging water up the hill, there was an eaves trough draining into a wooden rain barrel for the women of the house to use for washing their hair. Rainwater was especially good to make their hair shiny and soft. Sometimes, the barrel got little worms in it and Joe was tasked with carefully dipping them out.

After doing dishes, water went down the kitchen sink, through a pipe and elbow below the ground, and into a three-inch clay drain tile. The tile ran downhill and into the ditch. It was the only place where the dirt was damp all summer long and created a perfect environment for Joe to dig worms for fishing.

Carrying water for the wooden washing machine and doing the wash was a big chore. The machine had a long handle that had to be pushed back and forth to agitate the clothes. Young Joe was responsible for making sure the clothes got agitated really well. Fortunately, the few clothes they had weren't washed very often.

Another chore Joe had to do, involved churning the milk. The Guernsey cow was the source of the family's milk, two to three gallons a day. Mother poured the warm whole milk into a 20-inch-high crock to be carried down to the cool root cellar to store overnight. By morning, the sweet cream rose to the top. When there was enough cream, Joe churned it by hand. He started out pounding hard with the churn's long handle, and then when the butter started to coagulate, he tapped it with a softer touch until it formed into a ball. The family drank some of the leftover skim milk. Any soured milk was carried out to the chickens, and most of the butter was sold in town.

Making sure the cows got serviced was another duty. When one of the cows got in heat, it was no problem getting her to go to the neighbor's bull for a rendezvous. However, getting her back home was a much more challenging task. John led the cow and Joe walked behind with a switch to keep her motivated to walk in the right direction.

The field of alfalfa was cut several times a summer, raked by hand into windrows to dry, and days later loaded onto an old four-wheel buggy and then Joe dragged the buggy to the barn, where he pitched the dried hay into the loft. Joe truly had to work like a horse since they never owned one.

Another chore Joe often helped with was working at his father's smithy in town. His father taught him how to sharpen cultivator shovels and polish plowshares. Joe even learned how to run the hand-cranked drill press for tapping and making precision holes.

In addition to chores around the homestead and the smithy, Joe did whatever odd job he could find to bring in a little money. When he was old enough, he folded and delivered the *Des Moines Tribune*. Not only did he get a few cents for his work, he also got a free paper. At age eleven, he found a job milking cows before and after school for $3.50 a week. He had to tromp over to the neighbor's farm in the dark, light the kerosene lantern in the barn, and milk eight cows. He poured the heavy buckets full of rich, warm milk into the cream separator, which separated out the cream to be sold in town. The thin leftover milk was used by the family. He then repeated the chore in the evening.

One week the neighbor, who owned a profitable store in Linden, didn't pay him his wages for the week. Joe's dad was hopping mad and went right over to talk to him. "It isn't right to not pay when Joe is doing all that work for you, morning and night," Joe's dad snapped. Happily, Joe had his money the next day.

From the time Joe was twelve, he bought all his own clothes and whatever else he needed. He always gave some of his earnings to his dad, knowing he wouldn't get any back. Work, hard work, and helping out family were at the core of Joe's daily life and helped him grow into a responsible adult.

Food Gathering

Joe frequently was involved in finding food any way he could. Come springtime, he roamed the countryside, 2 to 3 miles in all directions from where he lived in search of his favorite spring treat. In April and early May, he'd start walking up and down the railroad tracks searching for rotten logs and signs of fungus. His search for the ridged morels yielded them by the three-gallon bucketfuls. At home, Joe filled the buckets with water and salt to soak the morels overnight, allowing all the little bugs to float to the surface. Then Mother sliced the mushrooms and fried them in rich butter. Joe remembered, "Geez, they tasted good. And what a delicacy!" Townspeople came in the spring to search for them, but Joe kept the treasured spots secret.

Joe also knew where to find the wild strawberry patch. Even though the berries were only one-quarter inch in diameter, they were so very sweet and delicious. Every once in a great while when he was little, Joe brought home a big pail of strawberries. His mother would say, "And thy cheeks are redder still, kissed by strawberries on the hill," and give him a peck on the cheek, one of her rare demonstrations of affection. She made divine strawberry shortcake for supper, which Joe loved. But when she made rhubarb dumplings, that was another story. Joe truly hated rhubarb dumplings; but as he remembered, "It was either that or starve." Mother never failed to stretch what little they had and make sure the family had something to eat.

Joe remembered picking gooseberries. They were disgusting alone, but were made a little more palatable when his mother mixed them with wild mulberries. Sugar was dear and not at hand much of the time. Dandelion tea in the summer made a change of pace from the usual drinks of milk and water.

Joe knew the woods well and brought home juneberries which tasted a lot like blueberries. His mother made them into delicious jam. Hickory nuts were gathered, but they took a lot of work to break open and get out of the shells. A not particularly good pear tree in the yard produced some fruit, but not much. In the fall, the apple tree along the lane yielded good eating apples toward September, and any not eaten were made into applesauce and then canned.

The black walnut trees in their yard produced a bounty of nuts. Joe used a hand-operated corn sheller to take off the green, mushy husks. It was a lot of effort to pick, hull, and then pull out the nut meats, and the work resulted in a black stain on Joe's hands that didn't wear off until January. After the bold-flavored black walnuts dried, they sold them for one dollar a bushel to the townsfolk.

When Joe grew older, he tinkered in his father's shop, trying to figure out an easier way to work up the bottomland for planting the garden. Joe's idea was to use a junked Chevy truck chassis with a five-speed transmission and connect it to another transmission. "That's not going to work," his dad asserted. But once completed, Joe's tractor had a very low gear range allowing it to move at a turtle's pace and made it exceptionally powerful. It efficiently pulled a single bottom plow for the garden. It was a sweet triumph for Joe to prove his dad wrong.

He used his self-made tractor to plant the bottomland where the ground was rich from being flooded during heavy rains. He planted watermelons, which he loved, and even planted peanuts one time. Unfortunately, the peanuts weren't a successful experiment. They were still soft and milky at the end of the season. It was the last time he tried raising peanuts.

Watermelons grew wonderfully big in the rich bottomland. Once ripe, the watermelon was put in the washtub and covered with cold well water until it cooled. They ate out the sweet, juicy heart without the seeds and threw the rind to the chickens. Watermelon was by far Joe's favorite summer treat.

Cucumbers were eaten fresh. But they were prolific, so the excess was packed into a large crock, covered with a brine of vinegar, water, salt, and fresh dill from the garden to make crunchy pickles.

Although he hated eating fish, Joe caught catfish for the "caviar," which was a valued prize his father dearly loved. He first had to catch goldfish minnows from the pond. Then he used them on a seine in the Mosquito Creek. The long lines with a stake on one side were thrown out with shorter baited lines every two feet. The catfish and light gray masses of eggs netted a big smile and a pat on the head from his father.

By August every year, the Mosquito Creek nearly went dry. In the rapids where the carp swam, the water got so low their backs would stick out of the water. Joe took a hoop off an old buggy wheel and covered it with wire mesh to make a net. He stood in the middle of the rapids, threw the net over the carp, and caught a lot. Carp weren't good to eat, but were fed to the chickens, and that made Mother happy.

Mother's kitchen became the center of activity in the fall where she canned almost everything from the garden and the family ate from the shelves of the root cellar all winter long. The bountiful cellar provided for special occasions too. Thanksgiving always meant a delicious meal. Mother bought two bananas to slice and share with all the family. At Christmas, Jell-O with a sliced orange graced the table. Mother did the best she could with what she had to feed the family all year through and to make holiday meals a special treat.

Hunting and Trapping

Joe had fond memories of another important duty he undertook which was trapping. At only four years old, he started his training. Rabbits and other food animals could not be wasted for practice; instead, his dad guided him to carefully bait and set a mouse trap.

Once he caught a fat mouse, his dad showed him how to take the knife and carefully skin it. The knife had to be very sharp to work on the skin of a mouse, which was quite fragile. As Joe recalled, "I learned to skin the leg around and up to and down the back, being careful on the stomach side, up to the ear. Then I cut close to the head, around the eyes, down to the nose, and one last cut. Rural living didn't allow anyone to be faint of heart or squeamish, no matter their age."

Joe carefully scraped the little mouse hide clean and pulled the skin onto the stretcher using small tacks to hold it tight. He let the skin hang to dry until stiff and then he began the process anew until the skills were mastered. Practice, practice, practice. Joe practiced and helped his brother John until he was a little older and could begin his hunting and trapping in earnest.

Joe admired his older brother John who was an excellent shot and could hit a rabbit in the head as it ran lickety-split, but he never liked the work coming after he shot it. According to Joe, John had a tender side. Fox dens were few and far between in the Iowa countryside, but one time, John caught a baby fox and put it in a cage. At night, the mother fox came into the yard and howled pitifully. It wasn't long before John turned the young kit loose to be reunited with its mother. When John graduated from high school and headed to Oklahoma to get a job on a ranch, Joe, at age nine, became the designated hunter and trapper of the family.

All Joe's older siblings except DeElda and Arlene had moved out to find jobs and try to make a living after they graduated high school. Goldie went to live and work as a domestic with the B. Rees Jones family when Joe was five. When he was eight, Echo left to work as a domestic. A scandal rocked the family when her father wrote the post master in a neighboring town and learned Echo was living with a married man twelve years her senior. According to Joe, "Dad was furious and completely disowned her." And now John was gone and DeElda, soon to graduate, would be off on her own. So, with a family of only five now and a new baby on the way, more than ever, Joe needed to help provide.

Joe loved Spot, his collie mix, who had been by his side since he was a tot. And Spot loved Joe. They roamed the hills and woods of the homestead and neighboring countryside together. In the fall, wherever Joe went Spot was always there, and was especially excited when he went hunting.

One of young Joe's first efforts to make money for the traps he needed for hunting was to go out in the summertime along the creek bank with his dog Spot and fill in groundhog holes with rocks. With the tunnels blocked, the groundhogs had only one tunnel to exit and he and his dog were often able to get a whole family at one time. A groundhog's scalp brought 25 cents, and the rest was great feed for Mother's chickens. Gophers' front feet brought 10 cents a pair. The neighboring farmers were happy to have Joe get rid of the destructive critters on their land. By the time he was in second grade, he had saved enough money for his own traps and was quickly proficient at running a trap line. The rabbits and squirrels Joe trapped supplemented the family fare.

Mosquito Creek
Taken by Jeff and Brandie Briggs

Joe, Jim, and Spot

There was one big squirrel with an especially bushy tail always running around the small workshop out back of their home and was quite tame. Joe's dad had a soft spot for that squirrel, and it was completely off limits. His dad warned him, "Don't you dare kill that squirrel or you'll be sorry. There are enough squirrels in the woods for you to get."

Rabbit stew was a delicious mainstay of the family diet. Since there was no refrigeration, Joe would hang the rabbit from a wire in a tree where no wild animals could get at it after he had cleaned and gutted it. The meat from a raccoon was not too bad either, especially mixed with sausage. However, because pork was expensive, the family only had ham or sausage on the rare occasion.

Ever inventive, Joe was able to figure out an easier way to catch rabbits. With a trap, he wouldn't have to waste his precious bullets, which cost a half cent apiece. He built a wooden box about six inches wide and nine inches tall, small enough to shove into a rabbit hole. At one end of the trap were rods and at the other end was a little gate on a pivot, opened so the rabbit could see all the way through to daylight. Once a rabbit tried to go out of its hole, the gate snapped down and the struggling wild, brown rabbit was caught.

The biggest challenge was finding rabbit holes, usually burrows taken over from groundhogs or skunks which required time. The big hill to the north was pasture, wide open, and a good spot. Joe, loaded down with the box traps, set them out in the evening after dark. Walking along the big hill, he had to be very careful because there was a hugep drop off down to Mosquito Creek. Up before the crack of dawn, Joe went out to check to see if he'd had any luck. He had a near accident when he lit a match to see what he'd caught and flicked it away. The dry pasture grass caught on fire and he had to hustle to stomp it out before the whole field went up in flames. When winter arrived, it was easier for Joe to follow tracks in the snow and know exactly where to place the traps, and he didn't have to worry about the pasture catching fire.

When Joe did catch a rabbit, he dispatched it by stepping on its head and pulling on its hind legs. Skinning a rabbit was done quickly, as the fur easily pulled off. Then Joe split the rabbit in two and checked the liver before anything else. Spots on the liver indicated the rabbit had tularemia, dangerous to humans. If it looked all right, he gave the guts to the chickens, rinsed the meat, and hung it in the tree. Everyone looked forward to Mother frying fresh rabbit with potatoes. Joe loved his mother's rabbit hash seasoned liberally with salt.

One crisp autumn day, Joe and his best friend, Gordon McConnell, went hunting rabbits in the woods near the homestead. Gordon quietly walked out in front of Joe, looking for game. All of a sudden, there was an explosive burst of sound. Gordon froze and turned white as a ghost. Joe's rifle had accidentally gone off. The next instant Gordon was raging mad. "Damn you, Joe! You about scared me to death!" he roared. He was so furious he made Joe take off his hat and give it to him. Gordon wadded it up, threw it on the ground, and proceeded to fill it with bullet holes. By the time he was done shooting, Gordon had settled down and the score was even.

Joe spent much of his free time in early fall preparing for trapping. He needed to build a huge fire and boil all his traps in black walnut hulls before setting them out. Of course, the black walnut nutmeats had to be laboriously picked out before boiling the hulls. The tannic acid in the hulls not only formed a layer of protection against rust on the steel traps, but also hid human scent. Even being careful, Joe's hands turned black during the process.

Once the season started, traps for muskrats were anchored under water all along the river. Joe learned a muskrat would go to the extreme of chewing off its foot to get out of a trap, but with the trap below the water line, the muskrat simply drowned. Joe was excited when he caught an otter whose velvety, brown fur brought exceptionally good money.

Joe also carried a .22 Stevens single-shot pistol when he checked his trap line. Once he found a raccoon in one of the traps. He took out his pistol and aimed. His heart broke as he saw a forlorn tear roll down its face, but he did what had to be done.

Joe's .22 Stevens single-shot pistol

Joe had two pairs of waders he used for trapping, his hip boots, and a pair going all the way to his waist. Whether there was a small hole or a big hole, Joe never threw them out, he simply patched them. Getting soaked with cold water just one time was enough to teach him that lesson.

Joe set his traps in the evening and returned the next morning to see what he had gotten. Spot always accompanied him. One time, Spot ran ahead and danced around a possum in Joe's trap. Joe skinned and cleaned it right there in the woods. The pelt was soft and supple. He built a fire and put the meat on a spit to roast. Soon however, the smell wafting up from the possum wrinkled his nose. Hungry, Joe tried to eat it, but it was just too disagreeable. Even Spot turned his nose up at the rank-smelling possum.

Joe hated to see the meat go to waste. He knew chickens loved possums so he took the remains home to his mother. She was pleased, because all the protein made the chickens lay an egg each day and turned the yolks a rich golden yellow. Of course, chicken feed was not something the Dew family spent money on. His mother occasionally did grind just a little ear corn for the chickens when there weren't enough scraps or possums, but even at a low of 12 cents a bushel, money for corn was dear.

One crisp fall day, Joe carried a possum down to the creek to drown it. It hung on by its long, thick, hairless tail curled snugly around his arm. The possum was playing dead but came to life when Joe walked through some tall, prickly thistles. As Joe recalled, "That possum clawed up my arm and was mad as all get out." He eventually got the hissing, wriggling varmint under control and finished the deed.

In the fall of the year from time to time, Joe shot a duck on the river. A goose was a rarity but made a savory meal. There were a few wild turkeys around Linden, seven miles west of Redfield. They were exceptionally hard to get and they would run like the devil the minute they heard the slightest sound. It was an uncommon treat when Joe outsmarted one and brought it home for the family dinner table.

Joe even caught the occasional bull snake. He quickly learned to discern the difference of coloring and patterning between rattlesnakes and bull snakes. As he closed in on one six-foot-long bull snake, it hissed and reared as if to strike. Joe distracted the snake with a stick, grabbed it, and it was quickly dispatched. The next step was to skin it and stretch the skin out on a long 7-inch-wide board. Once dried, he took a regular belt and pulled the skin over the outside, sewing it on to make himself a fancy snakeskin belt.

During trapping season, which lasted from mid-November to March, Joe got up early to check his trap lines before going to school. He pulled on his boots, grabbed a flashlight, and headed into the dark with Spot darting ahead to see what he'd managed to get. When Joe got home from school, he changed his clothes and went to the barn, where he skinned what he had hauled in before school and hung the catch on a line. Joe was careful to stretch each pelt to its maximum in order to get the best price when time to sell them rolled around.

With colder weather and thickening pelts, muskrat season opened November 15, and 15 traps were permitted. As he got older and more creative, Joe set 15 traps here, 15 traps there, and 15 in

34

other spots along the Mosquito Creek and Raccoon River. In a good season, he got 75 to 100 muskrats, fetching $1.50 each, and $2.50 for an especially big one.

Whenever Joe caught a rich chocolate-brown furred mink, only two or three a season, he was thrilled. Each one netted a whopping $20. He also got skunks and civet cats. Civet cats were the size of a small rabbit, with mostly black, short hair and a number of white spots. These critters smelled even worse than a skunk. Their pelts weren't very valuable, only $1.50 each, the same as possums.

By the end of muskrat season, the rivers and creeks froze over and it was time to trap skunks. There were three kinds of skunks: broad striped, medium striped, and narrow striped. Their thick fur was dyed and used for making coats. The narrow-striped skunks were worth the most. Once in a while, Joe got an almost completely black skunk, which brought top dollar. It wasn't long before he figured out how important it was to cut out the skunk's anal scent glands the very first thing. Another lesson Joe learned was to not throw the glands in the fire. When those glands hit the hot coals, the smell was dreadful and stunk up the whole area. Although skunks brought good money, they definitely had their downside.

One memorable day in sixth grade started out just as any other day, except Joe was running late.

"Joe!" yelled his mother. "Hurry up! You're going to miss the bus."

Leaves crunched under his feet as Joe ran to the three-room home, grabbed his lunch wrapped in newspaper, and headed down the long, rutted drive. Puffs of icy breath floated beside him as he ran as quickly as he could in his pinstriped overalls in the dim, dawn light to catch the bus, where he sat on the long bench running along the window.

The school bell rang just as Joe stepped into Mrs. Brown's classroom. She knew before she turned around something was wrong.

"Out of here this minute, Joe Dew," yelled Mrs. Brown. "Get to the principal's office right now!" Joe hadn't taken too much notice of anything unusual as he checked his traps in the morning.

"What on Earth?" exclaimed the principal as she turned to see and smell Joe all in the same instant.

"Down to the basement with you, Joe! Take your books with you. You'll do your studies down there today," muttered the principal as she frowned at Joe.

The basement wasn't too dreary and there was a chair next to the furnace, so it was nice and warm. It certainly was better than a mile walk home from school on that crisp fall day.

No sooner had Joe settled down than the furnace kicked on. The air intake swooshed the warm air up to the classrooms throughout the school. Soon the entire school was filled with the loathsome skunk smell which permeated every room on all four floors.

Windows were thrown open and students wondered what the cause of the disagreeable smell was. Years later, classmate Hazel Whitney recounted, "That was the day that Joseph Harold Dew disrupted our entire school." It was an event his classmates joked about years later at their 50th class reunion.

Trapping kept Joe busy most of the winter. Local people bought the pelts, but they didn't give a very good price. Sears Roebuck, one of the largest fur-buying companies in the country at the time, sent out an annual magazine, *Tips to Trappers*, which included information about their fur depot in Des Moines. Joe decided to drive to the big city and check it out. There was no set price of what they would give him, but they were fair and he put to use his fledgling skills at dickering to negotiate a good deal.

Joe's long hours and hard work trapping paid off. The capitol was only 30 miles away and with the Model T getting 25 miles per gallon and gas at 20 cents a gallon; it wasn't too expensive to drive there at all. He especially enjoyed the opportunity to eat a real restaurant lunch in a café for 75 cents when he made the trip.

Joe did get a few luxuries with his trapping money. Early on, he sent for a Jew's harp from the Sears Roebuck catalog. While in high school, he ordered a chromatic harmonica for $3.50 which was more expensive than the cheap ones for $1.50. It had more holes and a button, so it not only played a normal major scale, but with the button pressed in, Joe could play all the half-step notes in between. It was a lot of money, but he felt it was well worth the extravagance he afforded himself.

Jew's harp

Chromatic harmonica

The combination of the Depression and the lessening need for blacksmiths made for tough times. Joe's dad had to close his blacksmith shop in town when Joe was in the tenth grade. He moved his tools to their homestead, but what little work he got didn't bring in much. Joe carefully managed the money he got for his furs and held back enough for the next year's expenses for boots, traps, and his license. In addition to bringing a variety of food to the table in those difficult times, Joe helped out the family in any way he could.

Jim and Joseph at homestead shop

Curiosity

Curiosity and a sense of adventure were an innate part of Joe from the very beginning. When he was just a little tyke, his sister Goldie took him up the ladder to the small barn loft to play. One day when she was at school, Joe toddled out to the barn and climbed up in the loft all by himself. His dad looked out the shop window just in time to see Joe flying out the loft door. He almost had a heart attack as he ran to his son's side and scooped him into his arms. Fortunately, he was fine, but screaming bloody murder. Goldie felt awful when she got home from school and heard what had happened to her little brother.

Joe learned to drive in the days before a driver's license was required. At the tender age of six, he drove the old Model T truck up and down the lane. However, Joe's dad was none too happy when he veered off the lane and hit a stump. Another time at age eight, he came too close to the south end of the house and knocked off his mother's flower box. By the time Joe was twelve, he was regularly driving. His friend Lavern Sloan recounted, "Joe and I would often go to the junkyard and siphon gas off the junkers to get enough for some adventure. We always were able to find gas and someplace to go."

While out roaming the homestead with Lavern, they ran across a huge rock on the hillside near the good-sized ravine to the north of the house. Eager to learn what it was, Joe chipped off a chuck of the unusual, scaly, black rock, which was roughly two feet high, two feet wide, and 18 inches deep. He held a yardstick and Lavern took a picture of it. To determine what it was, Joe mailed the chunk to a government lab in Colorado. He was flabbergasted when he got a letter back and learned a large meteor had crashed right there on their property. A rock from the heavens! Joe stayed interested in the mysteries of the skies his entire life.

Joe and meteor

Wandering the woods at night, Joe learned the secret of foxfire. Kicking a rotted tree stump, Joe scooped up the bluish-green bioluminescent foxfire and took it home. Fungi rotted the wood and caused it to glow in the dark. There was no heat from the foxfire, but Joe broke off a chunk of wood, took it under the covers at night, and used it to read. The foxfire didn't last long but added mystery and wonder to fall nights.

Ever resourceful, Joe figured out a way he and his neighbor friend, Lester Chambers, could communicate. They got a book from the library and together studied the short and long dots and dashes of Morse code. Then at night, Joe sat on the hill by his house and sent messages with a flashlight to his distant friend.

Joe kept thinking of how he could put together a telegraph to use between his house and Lester's for even better communication. Using the coils from junked cars, he and Lester ran wire from the house, over the alfalfa field to the big black walnut tree, and down to the railroad track, following the top of the barbed-wire fence down into the timber. Joe shimmied up a tree to get the wire across the Mosquito Creek to the fence on the other side. They followed that up to the telephone pole, over to the fence, and on up to

Lester's house. They put the wire high to get across the gates so as to not cause any problems.

They each had a Model T Ford coil spark gap transmitter hooked to a battery. The signal went through the wire and made a static sound on the headphones they each had. Dot-dash, back and forth, back and forth. Sitting in their rooms at night, Joe and Lester honed their Morse code skills and had a great deal of fun.

Even though they didn't have phones, Lester and Joe figured out how to tie into the telephone line. They used it once in a while in the winter time to find out if they were going to have school or not.

Joe set aside some of his trapping money and sent for a liquid crystal radio kit, a "Little Tattler." As he fiddled with the tuner, nothing but static greeted his ears. He tried again in the evening and was excited to get Good Old XER country western tunes coming all the way from Mexico.

XER actually was the advertising brainchild of Dr. John Brinkley who, after being run out of Kansas, set up base in Del Rio, Texas, and located the 75,000-wattage border blaster radio station just across the Rio Grande River in Mexico. He eventually raised the wattage to a record high of 1,000,000 watts. Along with the country music, his station broadcasted medicine show programs, advertisements for cures for prostate problems, and the best sex cure of all time. For a whopping $750, you got Dr. Brinkley's infamous goat gland operation, a sure cure for impotence.

There were no government rules for broadcasting at the time, and the XER transmitting tower in Mexico was very powerful. The station was so powerful it could be heard all the way to Canada on a clear night. Joe fondly remembered, "I sure enjoyed listening to cowboy songs in the evening." Texas was a long way from Iowa, and he was quite excited he was able to pick up a radio station so far away. He did have to be creative making an antenna. He used the copper wire from junk car generators and ran the wire up a nearby maple tree to pick up the distant radio waves.

In 1933 when Joe was in his first year of high school, there was great excitement when his father bought a radio for the family.

Only problem was they never did have electricity out in the country. Joe's dad fiddled with the batteries for quite a while, but much to his consternation, he couldn't figure out how to hook up the three different-sized batteries and get the radio going. "There's no way to make this darn thing work," vehemently declared Joe's dad. Joe delighted in any opportunity to prove his dad wrong. And that's just what he did!

He set to work and hooked up the three batteries: a 6V battery, a 135V battery, and a 12V battery, and had the radio operating in short order. As good as that was, Joe's dad was perturbed Joe had been able to figure it out when he couldn't.

While in high school, Joe got a job at an alternator shop, a fix-it garage in Redfield. In trade for his work, the owner gave him an alternator that Joe set up with two windmills so he could recharge the radio batteries. He put one windmill on the house and located one atop the big hill. He was pleased with the windmills and the energy they generated for the family.

Joe atop house 1933   **Goldie and Mother by windmill on hill**

Having that radio provided the family with a great deal of entertainment. Now they could hear what was happening locally

41

and nationally. They listened to sports announced by Ronald Reagan from Des Moines. They listened seriously as FDR gave his Fireside Chats on how he was going to pull the nation out of the grip of the Great Depression. But Saturday nights were the best when they tapped their toes and forgot their troubles as they listened to the Grand Ole Opry.

Joe's curiosity and love of learning motivated him to explore the world around him. He was fearless in tackling all kinds of problems. He looked at any problem as a challenge and enjoyed trying to figure out a solution, which he usually did.

School Days

School provided Joe with many opportunities. At only four years old, he was excited to start first grade. He put on his stiff, new hickory stripe bib overalls Mother had ordered from the Sears Roebuck Catalog. One pair was for school and one pair was for going to the Methodist church on Sunday. Last year's short, patched pairs were for around home. Most everything the family bought was ordered from the catalog. Joe laughingly recounted, "When a new one arrived, we put the old catalog in the outhouse and used it for toilet paper. When the catalog got down to just the colored pages, it was time to get more catalogs."

Joe often had cornflakes with milk for breakfast. His mom carefully wrapped an egg sandwich for his lunch in the comic section to take to school. Off he walked down the lane with his brother and sisters to catch the bus for his first day in a class of 25 students. Joe was proud to be a country kid, although according to him, "The city kids looked down on all us kids from the country. We endured our fair share of being picked on and mean comments." Every day when Joe came home from school, he carefully took off his school overalls and shoes. Those new overalls weren't washed for several months.

John, Jim, Joe · Arlene, Jim, Joe

He never wore shoes at home until it got so cold he couldn't stand it anymore. Whenever the soles of his shoes wore thin, his dad used a cobbler machine at the blacksmith shop to put in nails and mend them with a heavy leather piece. Then he used stove blacking in a little bottle with a brush to make the shoes shine like new.

The school was right in the middle of Redfield, a peaceful rural town with a population of nearly 800. The first-grade classroom was on the lowest floor in the school and, miracle of miracles, there was a bathroom right in Joe's room.

Third grade class-Joe third from left in back row

43

By the time Joe finished second grade, he was doing so well his teacher, Miss Bailey, wanted to promote him to fourth grade. When asked, Joe's mother would hear of no such thing and vehemently refused to let her son jump a grade.

Joe's third grade teacher, Miss Sally Wells, was very prim and proper. She had a high school student, Harold Niblo, assigned to her class to do his normal training to become a teacher. During music one day, the eager young student teacher met with an accident. He had started cranking the classroom phonograph and caught the crank on his pocket. Unflustered, Miss Wells pulled out needle and thread and stitched his ripped pants, as the delighted third graders watched and giggled.

Family members were frequent visitors in the primary grades. Many mothers came to school and brought along their pre-school toddlers. Joe's classmate Hazel Whitney recounted, "I was really embarrassed when my younger brother Arnold came to school and my mother allowed him to sit with me." All was calm as the students worked on their lesson. That was until Hazel's young brother stood up, turned around and faced Joe, directly behind him, and sang out in a clear voice, *"You're a Yankee Doodle Dandy."* Lots of giggles, and a mortified Hazel turned redder than her hair.

In the spring, lunchtime meant picnics down by the river. The students made the hike of nearly a mile to Hanging Rock on the Raccoon River. They sat in the shade of the trees by the river eating their lunches. After emptying their lunch buckets, they scooped up handfuls of sand, filled their lunch buckets, and toted them back to school to replenish the playground sand box.

At the end of the year, the largest picnic was an all-school affair held at the Garrett Farm. All the students in the primary grades loved Mr. Niblo and invited him to go along. Tag, sack races, and competitions of all sorts kept the children busy and in high spirits. According to Hazel Whitney, "That year, a large number of the students in the primary grades had whooping cough but were permitted to go to this special event. With all the excitement and running, after they ate lunch, many "whooped" their food while the teachers and older students had to hold their heads."

In fourth grade, the big event every child looked forward to was going by bus to the great capitol city of Des Moines, 30 miles away. Joe had never seen the big city. When he sighted his first trolley car, classmates recalled he climbed on the seat and hung out the open bus window waving from sheer excitement.

Locust Street Bridge and Municipal Building, Des Moines, Iowa.

The eager children got to see the sights at the State Historical Building exhibits and the ornate Capitol with its shiny, golden domes. Riding on an elevator was something eight-year-old Joe had never done before. When it started going up, his eyes got big, and he grabbed the person's hand next to him, only to be startled the hand he grabbed was black.

At the Capitol, some of the girls wanted to go to the restroom, and Joe piped up he wanted to go rest with them. The teacher quickly explained to him it was just for girls. At noon, Joe sat on the sprawling lawn of the Capitol with his classmates and ate his lunch. The day flew by and quickly it was time to board the bus and make the trip back home. The superintendent, Mr. Frink, had come along on the field trip to chaperone the group. As the noisy busload of kids returned to Redfield, students snickered when he dozed off and began softly snoring. It was a most memorable trip for all.

Each year, classmate Beulah Dickey and Joe competed to get the top honors in the class. On a rainy, boring spring day in fifth grade, daydreaming Joe tried to decide on the best design for his paper airplanes he absent-mindedly sailed out the second-floor window, although being careful to not get caught by the teacher. Unfortunately, his rival, Beulah, had no qualms in marching up to the teacher's desk and tattling. The teacher sternly reprimanded Joe and sent him out in the rain to pick up all the papers in the school yard.

In the sixth grade, Miss Dennis introduced debate in English class. Learning skills in critical thinking and arguing any point of view was a lot of fun for Joe. He and several others often carried on the classroom debate through lunch, eating their cold lunch in the room and having a lively time.

It was in the sixth grade Joe came home on a chilly March day and was surprised to find he had a new baby brother, James Russell Dew. Jim was the only child a doctor had come to the house to help with the delivery. Mother was 43 years old when he was born. He was ten years younger than Joe and named after a family friend.

Mother and Jim 1931

Once seventh grade arrived, the school combined Joe's class with the eighth-grade class to form the junior high. Budget constraints made the combination of the two classes a necessity. Sixty students were a lot to crowd into one classroom. The teacher, Mr. Morrow, was not very well liked. He frequently read his newspaper as the students worked and they soon figured out his newspaper had a small peephole for spotting mischief in the classroom. More than once, Joe was the target of Mr. Morrow's keys. One time, he lobbed his keys at Joe for talking, but instead hit Hazel, who sat in the front of Joe. Years later, Joe reminisced, "It was a big job keeping all those kids in line and trying to teach them something."

It was in seventh grade Joe decided to compete in the school-wide spelling contest sponsored by the Des Moines newspaper. His nerves mounted as he made it to the final two and had to face Superintendent Frink's son, Edward, an eighth grader. Even though Joe was sure Edward missed his word, he felt he was unjustly given an opportunity to spell another one. Edward missed that word also, and Joe spelled it. There was no getting around it this time. Joe won the spelling competition by correctly spelling the word "promontory." When Joe arrived home, he proudly showed Mother his new dictionary and told her how he had won the competition by spelling the final word.

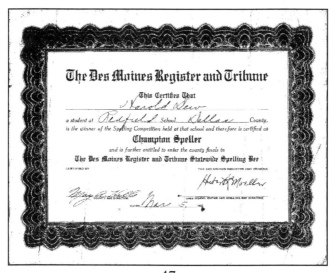

Throughout Joe's school years, heavy snows made "winter weather vacations" a common occurrence. High-school age bus drivers transported the country kids in Model T Ford chassis buses built with wooden bodies, no heater, and no lights. Two benches ran the length of the bus along each side wall with a narrow bench down the middle for the little ones.

Snow storms and blizzards made travel on country roads especially dangerous. "Some parents even insisted their children carry blankets on the bus, much to their embarrassment. Frost bite was not unheard of in those days," mused Joe's classmate Hazel Whitney. With the coming of spring and melting snow came mud vacations. According to Beulah Dickey, "Even when the buses were running, we would get stuck on the muddy, gravel road and have to walk the last mile to school."

Fall and the first day of high school arrived with Joe's class increasing to include a number of rural grade school graduates. These students had to pass county exams to be eligible to enter the Redfield School. Some came on buses, others had their own transportation thanks to their parents, and some boarded with local townspeople. A roller-skating initiation party was planned for the freshmen. Mr. E. E Reynolds offered to let the class use his empty building in downtown Redfield for the event. As much as he would have liked to have gone, Joe decided not to. He thought the 15 cents to get in was too dear.

Joe was well-liked and active in high school. As Hazel Whitney's younger brother Arnold said, "Most everybody in the school knew Joe. He was well-spoken and we considered him fair-minded and thoughtful of others." Freshman year, Joe was elected vice-president of the class and in tenth grade, he was elected president. The school offered three courses of study: normal training for teachers, college preparatory, and commercial. Joe's older brother John had completed the commercial program. "His skills at shorthand and stenography were awfully good," remarked Joe. Classmates Beulah and Hazel chose normal training and were excited at the prospect of being able to teach in a country school upon graduation from high school. Joe had no doubts he wanted to complete the college preparatory program.

Redfield Consolidated School built in 1923

Joe 1935

Upon arriving in school, students stopped to hang their coats and toss their lunches on the shelves outside the assembly hall. Each morning, there was a brief assembly before the principal dismissed students to their classes.

As leader of the class, Joe had decided on a plan for assembly to deal with the physics teacher, Mr. Speas, who was constantly disrespectful of his students. The final straw had been when Mr. Speas insulted Gordon McConnell, Joe's best friend. Joe had read in the *Des Moines Tribune* about a successful strategy used by General Motors workers. Their sit-down strike in Flint, Michigan, in 1936 resulted in the successful organization of the union. Joe made a plan and convinced his classmates to follow through. During the morning assembly, when Miss Dalton, the respected principal, called physics, the students just sat quietly instead of going to class.

Heavyset Mr. Speas stomped into the assembly inquiring why his students weren't coming. Miss Dalton shook her head in disappointment at the students' approach, but it got her attention and the problem with Mr. Speas was finally resolved.

There were lots of extracurricular activities possible for students attending Redfield High School. Miss Hopley's English classes put on school plays. Joe had the lead in a number of the plays, including *Spring Fever*, *A Birds' Christmas Carol*, and a mystery, *The Green Phantom*. His ready ability to memorize came in handy learning the lines.

In an operetta, Joe played the lead as a dashing pirate and wore hip boots. He clearly rang out in song, "I'm a mesmerizing son of a very remarkable man." In this romantic comedy, Joe got his fair share of laughs as well as accolades for his singing.

The junior class play was a mystery titled *The Blue Bag*. Unbeknownst to the audience, the lights had failed due to a storm. Fortunately, the play began on schedule with each actor entering on cue carrying a candle. The first act ended in this manner and the stage became well-lit by the time all actors and candles made their entrance. The final curtain came down to a standing ovation, just as the power was restored.

Joe was also active as a tenor in the boys' glee club, boys' quartet, mixed chorus, and mixed quartet. Their groups performed between acts during *The Blue Bag*, with Joe also playing a harmonica solo.

In the mixed quartet was Joe's girlfriend, Jean Meyers, a soprano. Joyce Walker, alto, and bass, Charles Straud, the preacher's son, finished out the quartet. After their quartet won the local competition, their music teacher, Miss Ada Maxon, loaned Joe her car, a 1930 Ford, to drive the group across the border to Missouri to perform in the next level of competition, which they happily won.

Joe in Miss Maxon's car

Sports

By 11th grade, Joe decided he wanted to be on the football team. Joe's mother didn't want him to play, because his older brother had broken two ribs when he played. She definitely did not want to see Joe hurt. However, Joe was determined. So, when the season came around, Joe stayed after school and joined the team along with his good friend, Don McKray. As Joe reminisced, "In those days, if you wanted to be on the team, you were. We played and practiced in the grassy field right behind the school."

Country living, hunting, and hard work made Joe as strong as an ox, and he was a welcome halfback on the Redfield High School football team in the 11th and 12th grades. Wearing helmets was made mandatory the first year Joe played. In those days, there was just one team, and the players had to play both positions for offense and defense. Joe recalled, "The padding was a heck of a lot less than today, and there was definitely not as much glory." Joe fondly recalled his coach as a good guy who always told Joe and his teammates to just go out on the field and have fun.

When the Redfield Bulldogs in their dark blue jerseys went to play the rival team in Casey, they were surprised to find a playing field in far worse shape than theirs. It was a big, grassy cow pasture. More than once, Joe and his teammates slipped on the cow pies and got smeared with the gooey stuff. That didn't stop Joe. He simply wiped himself off and got back in the game.

In a particularly close game with their biggest rival, Dexter, the coach told Joe and Don to take out the right defensive end. Joe went on one side and Don on the other. They squeezed the right end between them and ran with the struggling player off the field. The crowd cheered as the field opened up for their quarterback to carry the ball over the goal line, pushing Redfield ahead to win the game. There was no end to the good-natured razzing Joe and Don took the next week in school for their unique play.

Romance made for an exciting play at one Redfield home football game. Joe's friend, Don, got along with all the girls. In fact, one special girl promised Don if he made a touchdown, she would give him a kiss. But as the game progressed, it looked pretty bleak for Don making a touchdown. In the last quarter, Joe caught a pass and headed for the goal line. Always one to look out for his friends, Joe lateraled the ball to Don. The crowd cheered as Don took the ball in for a touchdown winning the game and a kiss. As Joe reminisced, "It sure was a wonderful game that night."

Joe's mother worried more about injuries in football than basketball. However, the year Joe joined basketball proved to have the most serious consequences. In a highly contested game, Joe got jabbed with an elbow right in his nose and started bleeding heavily. It hurt like the devil. He went home "pretty darn sore", with bruising beginning to show. His mother immediately realized his nose had been broken. "No son of mine is going to look like a beat-up boxer with a crooked nose!" she sternly admonished Joe.

The next morning, Mother sent Joe, against his protests, to the doctor in town. He took the railroad tracks, shortening the chilly walk to only a mile. The doctor took one look at Joe and ordered him to sit down. Without any kind of anesthetic, he forced the tips of the cold metal forceps into each nostril and yanked Joe's nose as hard as he could back into place. How painful! Joe walked the mile on the tracks back home, albeit bruised and sore, but with a straight nose, thanks to his mother's insistence.

Life was challenging growing up in rural Iowa, especially with limited money. Joe worked hard, studied hard, and found a lot of enjoyment in everything he did. He faced his challenges as they came and kept a positive attitude in his ability to meet those challenges.

Joe's Further Education

Joe Dew High School Graduation 1937

Graduation and Possibilities

Graduation day finally arrived, and with it a world of very limited possibilities. At age 17, Joseph Harold Dew and his 40 fellow classmates proudly walked to the stage in their caps and gowns to receive their diplomas from Redfield High School. Joe felt a sense of accomplishment, tempered by worry about how he was going to save enough money to realize his dream of going to college.

Jobs in Iowa were hard to come by with nearly a 25% unemployment rate throughout the country, even for a hard worker like Joe. But thankfully during the summer of the year he graduated, he found a job on the Purviance farm 20 miles from home. He took meals with the family and slept upstairs in his own room.

In exchange for a room, meals with the family, and $35 per month, Joe slopped hogs, milked cows, and tackled any other chore Farmer Purviance wanted done. Up at the crack of dawn, chores before breakfast, and working until the sun set six days a week. On Sunday, he was free after he finished the morning chores taking care of the animals.

Farmer Purviance felt the pinch of the times too and knew he needed to utilize as much of his land as possible. He put Joe to work on the wetlands, hand-digging trenches with a spade to lay clay tile in an effort to drain the wetlands and make them farmable. Once that job was completed, Joe ran the noisy old Farmall tractor to cultivate the weeds in the tender, green rows of corn. Those were long hours and heavy work, but Joe, ever frugal, managed to save for college.

The fall of 1937, Joe packed his bag for college, eager to begin working toward a degree in mechanical engineering. His summer work and savings were enough to pay the $90 tuition and have enough left for books at Iowa State College in Ames over 60 miles from home.

A country neighbor, Mr. Barnett, who had moved to Ames and gotten a job with the Iowa Road Commission, let Joe and his friend

Gordon McConnell rent an unheated attic room for $3.50 per week. The only glimmer of heat was from the chimney going through their room. Even with a bit of heat, a glass of water would freeze by Joe's bedside. The room was halfway between the town and college, right by a cinder path which ran along the train tracks. Joe splurged and spent $5 for a used bike to get around.

To make ends meet, Joe found two jobs. Mr. Gittigankis, his boss at Tom's Café, was Italian-Greek and a very good cook. Joe washed, dried, and stacked dishes every night until midnight. Sometimes, he carried food out to the customers. From time to time, he even cooked. Joe especially disliked cleaning the grill late at night with lye mixed with rancid cooking oil. One time while scrubbing the grill, he got a gash on the back of his hand which became badly infected. He waited a whole weekend to get treated at the college infirmary, because the local doctor was going to charge him $3, much more than he felt he could afford. Fortunately, it wasn't a fatal mistake to wait.

Mr. Gittigankis didn't pay Joe, but he earned his board. His second job found him at the college library shelving books. Even with two jobs and working a lot of hours, he barely scraped by. The long hours and late nights took a toll on his grades. He'd been an A student in high school, even graduated third in his class, but in college and taking six classes, he was struggling. He had to drop Chemistry and only got Cs and Ds in his remaining classes of Composition, Algebra, Drawing and Projection, Engineering Problems, and Physical Education. With a D in Algebra, he would have to retake the class and pay for it a second time. Joe was getting an education in more ways than one.

Challenging 1938

By winter term, Joe didn't have enough money to continue, and reluctantly returned home. He got a job in the butcher shop owned by Claude Diddy, who also owned the drug store in Redfield. He caught on quickly how to cut meat and grind hamburger and sausage. At home he quickly got up early before work to run his trap lines. All the while he was hoping he would be able to earn enough money to go back to college.

Deciding to change his major to electrical engineering, Joe headed back to Ames to resume his college classes in the spring, staying again with his friend Gordon. Gordon struggled with his classes and girl problems. Frustrated and out of money, Gordon dropped out of school before spring term ended. Joe made it to the end of the term, completing all his classes, but with grades so low in Chemistry (D) and Engineering Problems (C) he would have to repeat them if he continued in his major.

Happily, at the end of spring term, Joe found a steady job for the summer working for a farmer for $1 per day and room and board. When payday came, the farmer hung his head and hesitantly said, "I'm sorry, I just can't pay you."

Joe then made the decision to head west and try to find work. He jumped a train, and after numerous disappointments found a job on a ranch in Colorado. It was hard work six days a week. Joe slept on a cot in the barn at night with the rest of the crew and got meals, but did not earn much pay.

Joe recalled there were days working on the ranch when the dust blotted out the midday sun. One day while out working, Joe saw a dust devil twisting his way. Curiosity got the better of him as he wondered what one would feel like and ran toward it rather than away from it. It was more violent than he expected, carrying him along and knocking him around for quite some time. In retrospect, he thought he hadn't been very smart. "It was a wonder I wasn't killed," he reflected.

Another day working on a fence, he ran into a whopping big rattlesnake. It reared up, hissed, and threateningly rattled its tail at him. Joe took his work boot off, threw it at the deadly snake, and got the heck out of there. Joe had hated snakes ever since his first run-in with one on the homestead. He was relieved when the end of the season came so he could head back home to see family and start his fall trapping.

Back to College Spring 1939

Trapping through the winter allowed Joe to save enough money to return to Iowa State College for spring term, where he stayed on a cot for $3 a week in his Aunt Belle's musty cellar in Boone, 15 miles west of the college. His Aunt Belle taught school and lived with her close friend, Irene Clark, also a teacher. To supplement their income Aunt Belle also raised chickens and sold the eggs. She didn't provide any meals, so Joe went back to the same café he had worked at his freshman year. They knew Joe, liked him, and were happy to get him back, paying him in meals. He also got a job again at the library shelving books.

Aunt Belle and friend Irene

Joe looked around for better transportation than his bicycle for the long ride to campus and got a Harley Davidson motorcycle for just $45 after expertly dickering down the price. However, he hit a snag when he went to buy a license. The plate was expired and Joe didn't have the $25 needed to get a new one. Joe just couldn't afford that. He left the office muttering to himself. He talked to his dad who advised him to go see the uncle of one of his customers who worked in the license department. Joe looked him up and happily was able to get the license for a much more reasonable $3. Joe was in business. He used the Harley to go back and forth, riding on the cinder path that ran next to the railroad tracks and was a fast shortcut to campus.

One day on his way to college in the pouring rain, Joe had a flat tire on his motorcycle. He took the inner tube out, got it blown up, and finished the run to college. According to Joe, "People were more self-sufficient in those days. It wasn't easy, I'll tell you that, but we did what we had to do." Unfortunately, he ran into some misfortune when his Harley skidded on the way home in the rain and he flew off. He wrecked not only the Harley, but his body as well. He badly dislocated his thumb, an irritation bothering him his entire life.

Joe recounted stories of several of his college professors who were especially memorable. One day his psychology professor asked for several volunteers to be hypnotized. After going into a trance, a number of students began barking like dogs. Another student felt the pain of being burned by a non-existent cigarette. "I wouldn't have believed it if I hadn't seen it with my own eyes!" recalled Joe. The unusual demonstration made Joe a believer in the power of hypnosis.

Another professor he really liked was his undergraduate math professor John Vincent Atanasoff. While at Iowa State, Atanasoff developed the world's first automatic electronic digital computer. Joe later learned Atanasoff left Iowa State to work on the atomic bomb tests in the Pacific during World War II. After the war, Atanasoff developed a method and mechanism for sweeping for underwater mines. Although Atanasoff was an impressive teacher, Joe struggled with all the high-level math classes he had to take.

Spring term, Joe did poorly in Analytical Geometry. In fact, he failed it. His grades weren't as good as he would have liked in most of his classes, and his progress toward a degree was slow. He had only been able to complete three terms since high school graduation, and with disappointing grades. Juggling school and jobs to earn enough money to eke by was a constant challenge.

Back in Redfield after spring term, Joe and his two good friends Gordon McConnell and Lavern Sloan discussed their options for the summer. With few jobs in the area, they decided to hitchhike to Los Angeles and see what work they could find. According to Lavern, "We didn't really have any illusions about finding great jobs there; we just wanted to see the country."

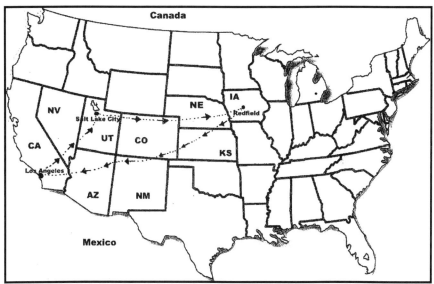

Trip to California car wash and Salt Lake City 1939

The trio, known as the three musketeers by their high school classmates, hitchhiked over 1,600 miles to the California coast. They found jobs at a car wash on Glendale Avenue in Los Angeles. At night they could see the distant Hollywoodland real estate development sign with its three-foot-wide by five-foot-high letters. It was quite a show at night with 4,000 light bulbs outlining the letters. The jobs were hard work, six days a week, but they made enough to pay for a back room right at the car wash with three cots and an inside toilet, and had a little money left over for food.

Joe was given a waterproof outfit and steam cleaned engines while the other two washed cars. Joe was a little awestruck when Lana Turner's chauffeur dropped off her car to be thoroughly cleaned. Of course, Joe knew Lana Turner. She was MGM's glamorous and sexy "Sweater Girl." According to Joe, "When the chauffeur came back to pick up Lana's car, he glared at me, lifted the hood, carefully put on a pair of white gloves, and ran a finger over the engine. And I'm proud to say there wasn't a drop of dirt to be found."

On their Sundays off, the three hitchhiked 30 miles to the beach. The Pacific Ocean was terrific. The waves and the salt-water taste along with the young people who yelled blatantly disrespectful comments made it an unforgettable experience for these naïve Iowa country boys. They even had a chance to sightsee on Rodeo Drive. What a good time they had!

After the car wash job, the three decided to head their separate ways. Joe hitchhiked north to Salt Lake City, Utah. He was intrigued by the soaring spires of the Mormon Temple framed by the mountains in the distance. Joe recalled, "I was hoping to go in, but was disappointed when I tried the door to the temple and found it firmly locked."

693 The Mormon Temple, Salt Lake City, Utah

He was stunned when he went into a restaurant called the Round Table and the meal was only 35 cents. Joe's eyes got big and he nearly started drooling when he sat down at the counter and saw all the food rotating in a continuous loop past the customers.

Dinner was meat, potatoes, and bread going round and round with plenty of desserts. He was utterly amazed he could fill up his plate with as much as he wanted as many times as he wanted. And he did!

When he left and started hitchhiking through Salt Lake City, a policeman stopped him. "Where are you going to sleep tonight?" the officer tersely asked him.

Joe politely replied, "I sure as heck don't know." Joe was a little leery, but the policeman took him down to the jail and let him sleep in an unlocked cell. He was grateful to have a safe place to spend the night and a decent bed to sleep on.

Joseph and Edna Dew

Home sure looked good that crisp, fall day when Joe jumped off the train as it chugged by the homestead. Seeing his family and being home brightened Joe's spirits. Jim was nine now. Mother and dad seemed the same as always. Although it was good to go adventuring and see new places, there was no place like home for Joe.

There weren't many jobs around with unemployment over 17 percent, but Joe got busy with his trap line, helped his dad at the blacksmith shop and around the homestead, trapped, and did whatever odd job that came along to save up money through the fall and cold, winter months.

Joe fretted on how he could make more money. He still hadn't been able to save enough to pay for spring term at college. When he saw a flyer in town advertising for farm workers, he determined he would head out west for the spring wheat harvest. There were simply no other jobs to be found locally. He packed his meager belongings in his duffle bag and jumped on the train to head west and work his way across the Central Plains following the ripening wheat all the way from Texas to Canada.

Hot, sweaty, backbreaking days. Nights in a barn or a haymow under the stars with other workers, entertaining them with a song or two on his harmonica. Joe had never seen anything like the expansive wheat fields of the Great Plains.

After the binder cut the wheat, Joe and the crew of harvesters bundled the grain into sheaves which were tied automatically. Then the sheaves were lined up in windrows. Next came the task of taking ten to 15 sheaves and making the bunches into large circular shocks. It took Joe some time to become skilled in making the sheaves. The shocked wheat was left with the tops branched out in order to shed the rain off the wheat heads. With most of the grain heads on top, the wheat was exposed to the open air and sun to dry.

Wheat harvest
North Dakota Institute of Regional Studies

From all the work, Joe had blisters on his blisters. His big hands had rough calluses more than an eighth of an inch thick. According to him, "When I rubbed my hands together, it sounded like rubbing together a couple of rasps that were grating against each other." Those thick calluses remained all his life.

Joe worked ten to fourteen-hour days, six days a week, under the hot sun, with a pitchfork in his hands, tossing the shocks of wheat onto a flatbed wagon with a rack. He was so strong he broke several pitchfork handles with the heavy loads of grain he could pick up. The farmer remedied the problem by adding a long pipe over Joe's pitchfork handle. Eventually, Joe was assigned to drive a team of horses. He made every corner as square as possible when making turns and easily mastered backing up the binder. It was a difficult task, but one he did well. He maneuvered the team expertly and cut every single stalk of wheat. He was a hired hand the farmers liked having on their crew.

Harvest lasted the entire summer and spanned the breadth of the country. The last farm Joe worked on was 15 miles from Canada, not too far north of Minot, North Dakota. The weather was turning cool as fall arrived. Harvest was finished. Time to move on.

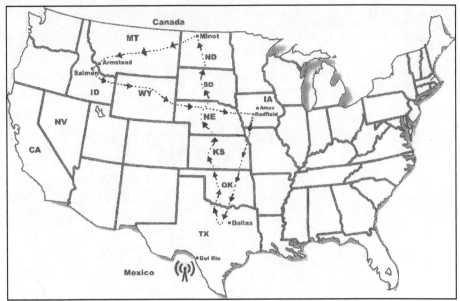

Wheat Harvest and the Great Divide 1940

Joe made his way further west, taking whatever odd job he could find. South of Dillon, Montana, in the small, dusty town of Armstead was the abandoned narrow-gauge Gilmore & Pittsburgh Railroad crossing over the mountains to Salmon, Idaho. Joe and another fellow, an out-of-work lawyer, got some provisions and ammunition and decided to make the 100-mile trek over the Great Divide. They took along a little food, but not much, being confident they would be able to get some food along the way.

It was arduous hiking in the high mountain air and it wasn't long until Joe was feeling darn hungry. He had hoped to shoot a rabbit, but spotted nary a one. He finally spied a scrawny hawk circling, took aim, and hit it. He plucked off the feathers, gutted it, and boiled it in a pot with water from the nearby stream. He and the lawyer managed to get a little meat and nourishment.

Although the mountainous countryside was breathtakingly beautiful, it was an arduous hike and getting colder the higher they went. They made close to 25 miles each day and were anxious to get back to civilization.

According to Joe, "After several days, we ran completely out of food and at such a high elevation, there just wasn't anything to shoot. We were on the verge of starving when we came across a poor family living in a run-down cabin along the tracks. Thankfully, the family generously shared what little food they had." With the small meal, Joe and the lawyer had enough energy to make the push to Salmon, Idaho, where a decent meal awaited them.

Bannock Pass-Great Divide 7,684 feet
Public domain

Arriving in Salmon, Joe and the lawyer ran into an old-timer who was going prospecting for gold. They decided to buy some pans, the miner's basic tool, and tag along with him. They followed the picturesque winding road out of town that ran along the broad Salmon River.

They chatted with the old-timer as they hiked along, finally turning onto a small road. According to the old-timer, there was an abandoned gold mine, which the locals called the Glory Hole, to the west and up in the mountains. They trudged along the mountain road, but had neglected to take any water with them. As Joe recalled, "We were so thirsty we considered flagging down a passing car and asking if we could drain some water from their radiator."

At last, they came to a rushing stream where a few old prospectors were hoping to strike it rich. After getting a drink and dropping off their bags, the lawyer and Joe grabbed torches and went along with one of them into the rickety old mine tunnel. They went deep into the mountain following a small track used by the railcars. The prospector stopped and cast light on the roof of the tunnel, illuminating a huge crack. According to Joe, "When the lawyer fella saw that crack, he got scared and hightailed it out of the tunnel lickety-split."

The prospector took Joe farther back to where they were hoping to pick up where the vein had run out. Joe hung around only until a load of rock was loaded and pushed it out.

In the glow of the campfire later, the lawyer and Joe discussed things and decided to move on. They picked up their few belongings the next morning and continued until they came to a ramshackle, deserted cabin. The only thing of interest and possible value at the cabin was a sluice box with rotted gunny sacks tacked to the bottom. Miners had ingeniously rigged a little rapids going out the end and the gold, being heavier, dropped down, getting caught in the fabric of the coarse gunny sack.

Joe built a fire and cautiously pulled the old sack loose. He burned the sack, took the ashes down to the creek and sure enough, there was some gold. He scooped the shiny flakes into a tobacco pouch and shoved it in his pocket. Having no more luck, they eventually gave up. Joe only ended up with the gold from the ashes, which he took to the assayer's office and was told there wasn't enough gold to bring any money.

It was getting on toward winter and Joe decided it best to head home. Hitchhiking was slow and unreliable for long distances, but better than walking. Riding the rails, although faster and covering more ground had its hazards. "Hanging under the train positioned on a board was especially risky, but so was leaping into an empty freight car as it picked up speed. Riding on top was especially precarious," according to Joe.

On one occasion when Joe jumped in one of the train cars, there was a lot of dry cement scattered over the floor. Exhausted and perspiring, he lay down to take a nap as the train rumbled along.

When he woke up, his clothes were stiff and uncomfortable where the concrete dust had hardened.

At another stop, Joe ducked under a boxcar just in time to miss being seen by the train bull. These bulls were brutal guards hired by the railroads to make sure only paying customers rode. Another fellow wasn't as fortunate. Joe heard the bull yell at him, followed by the loud conk of a club. As he watched through a crack, he saw the man drop unconscious to the ground. "You better believe I was scared," recalled Joe.

Joe happily jumped off the train at the homestead, but sad news awaited him. His dear sweetheart of a sister DeElda had been warned by the doctors a second pregnancy would be too much for her, and it was. She died at 25 of a cerebral hemorrhage on May 26, 1940, shortly after Joe had headed west.

Joe was heartbroken when his dad told him. It was with a heavy heart he visited her grave in the East Linn Cemetery just a few miles from their home. (DeElda's young son John Kitterman grew up to get his doctorate degree in physics and become a college professor and director of scientific research at South Dakota State University in Brookings, South Dakota.)

Taken by Jeff and Brandie Briggs

DeElda, son John, Howard

WIFE OF ARMY MAN DIES HERE

5/26/40

Mrs. Howard Kitterman, 25, wife of a first-class private at the Fort Des Moines army post, died Thursday night at the army post hospital.

Death was caused by a cerebral hemorrhage. Mrs. Kitterman had been a resident of Des Moines or Fort Des Moines eight years. She lived at 206 E. Leland ave.

Surviving are a son, John Howard; her parents, Mr. and Mrs. J. L. Dew of Redfield, Ia.; three brothers, John, Harold, and James, all of Redfield; and three sisters, Mrs. Echo Custer of Twin Falls, Idaho, Mrs. Arline Pruitt of LeClaire, Ia., and Miss Goldie Dew, Des Moines.

Services are to be at 2 p. m. Saturday at White's Funeral home. Burial will be at Redfield.

John, Dad, Goldie, Jim, DeElda, Mother, Arlene, Joe

70

World War II

Joe Dew

The Coming War

The newspapers had been full of reports of the ongoing tensions in the world. Japan attacked China in 1937, and by 1939 strained relations between the United States and Japan, along with improvements in the ability of bombers to travel longer distances, led to concerns about Alaska and its strategic significance to the country. On April 25, 1939, Congress approved expanded construction of defense facilities on the Kodiak Naval Reservation, a very isolated area.

Not having enough money to go back to college and unable to find work after returning home, Joe read about the work to be done in Alaska. He decided to go north with the hope of making some big bucks. John was having trouble getting good paying work too, so his dad told Joe to take John along with him. But Joe, who had been on the bum quite a bit, sharply snapped, "I'm not going to take care of him!" Relishing the memory, Joe said, "Dad about laughed his head off."

Joe made his good-byes, packed his duffle bag, and rode the rails to Seattle. He bought the cheapest ticket for $17.50 on the 350-foot steamer SS *Alaska* for the over 2,000-mile journey along the coast of Canada to his destination in Alaska. In steerage, he was in the bowels of the ship on the lowest deck. The waves hitting the front end felt like he was being hit by a sledgehammer as he lay in his bunk next to the chilly wall. Meals were served at tables bolted down, with chains clipped onto the plates.

SS *Alaska*

As the ship passed through the inland passage between Ketchikan and Juneau, Joe heard the captain joking, "We never go through at low tide." He told of a British captain who made the mistake of pushing through at low tide, stating snobbishly, "The King's navy waits for no tide." The British ship had scraped bottom and grounded. Everyone got quite a chuckle out of the captain's story.

Arriving in Anchorage on the Alaskan mainland, Joe took the long ferry ride to Kodiak, whose name came from the Inuit word "Kadiak," meaning island. It was a massive undertaking to build a base when the beginning population on Kodiak Island was just over 400, with no telephones, no electric lights, no sewers, no bank, no hospital, and in a rugged, mountainous, and heavily forested area. The population burgeoned to over 20,000 with the construction, and the island later became the major staging area for the World War II North Pacific U.S. operations. From roads to barracks to military installations, everything had to be built. Siems-Drake was in charge of constructing a submarine base and housing for personnel. In order to even be considered for the job, Joe had to first join the labor union.

His initial job for the civilian contractor, Siems-Drake Puget Sound Construction Company, was dirty work, digging trenches to help build a road from the city of Kodiak to the base, which was 7 miles away. The route for the road was above sea level with only a few feet of soil covering solid rock. Joe reflected, "My job was to dig a trench for the jackhammers and be careful to make it only wide enough for the jackhammer to fit in." The work was difficult and made even more so because the crew was always working on an incline. When the volcanic ash left from a 1912 eruption of Mount Novarupta mixed with frequent rains, it created a covering of mud, making the task even more onerous. The arduous work was accompanied by the steady boom of crews blasting rock. That was an extremely dangerous job and paid much better than Joe's. However, he had no interest in risking his life, and was more than content with $5.15 an hour.

Joe worked on building roads for over a month when he had an opportunity to become a carpenter's apprentice. He had a little experience sawing boards and cutting right angles. It paid more money, so he took the job working on building barracks. It wasn't long before he was able to put in an eightpenny nail with no more than three blows. One chilly day while working, the foreman asked Joe, "What do you want to do with your life?"

"Well," Joe replied, "I sure don't want to be a carpenter." The next day, Joe was summarily transferred to the "mud gang," digging foundations for houses. "It doesn't pay to be totally honest," mused Joe. "It was a hard life lesson."

Newspapers even far north in remote Alaska carried accounts of the expanding war in Europe and Asia. Joe had to go to Kodiak and sign up for the draft when the first peacetime conscription in the history of the United States was signed into law on September 16, 1940, by Franklin Roosevelt for all men aged 21 to 36. While there, he stopped at the Sears Roebuck and ordered a very nice leather jacket. He was disappointed it hadn't arrived by the time he had to leave for Iowa.

Working boat Joe rode on

Once he made the decision to go home, Joe snagged a ride on a working boat heading to the mainland, over 200 miles away. Shortly after the boat pushed off, Joe realized there was a problem.

The captain and all the crew, except for the cook, were drunk. By good luck, the cook knew enough of what needed to be done and got the boat safely to the mainland. Joe stepped off at high tide right onto the dock, leaving his bag and carpenter's tools on the boat while he went to check out the town. When he returned, three hours later, the tide had gone out. He had to make a treacherous climb 22 feet down a slippery, slimy ladder to retrieve his belongings.

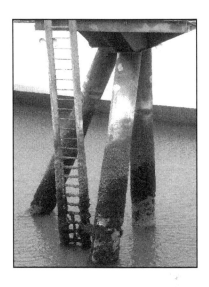

From there, Joe booked passage to return to the Lower 48 in steerage, again the least expensive ticket. This time, his spot in steerage was at the back of the boat, behind the engine room, noisy as all get out, but cheap. He had no interest in passing time gambling on the ship, but a lumber purchasing agent he met did. The agent had made a lot of money and was living high in first class. It wasn't long until the agent gambled away all the money he had made while in Alaska. Joe shook his head at the folly of the agent.

Docking in Seattle, Joe then hitchhiked over 250 miles to Hermiston, Oregon. With his previous experience, Joe quickly got a construction job building concrete ammunition bunkers at the Umatilla Ordnance Depot. The once lonely desert village with blowing sagebrush was now a bustling boomtown. Late spring with mild, dry, sunny days and cool nights was quite a change from the rainy wilds of Alaska. Joe joined over 7,000 who were working night and day to create the world's largest munitions depot for the impending war.

Joe wiped his brow as he surveyed the vast expanse of munitions igloos ready to house 2000-pound-blockbuster bombs for use in aerial bombings. He sighed, knowing this war would be a big one. Working hard and spending little, Joe pocketed $100 a week at the grueling construction job. It was here Joe got the news of the horrific attack on Pearl Harbor, December 7, 1941, and the declaration of war on Japan one day later. He packed his few belongings and headed home. Hitchhiking and riding the rails helped him hold on to the money he had worked so hard for.

Ready for War

Back in Redfield, Joe was happy to see the folks, but dismayed when he saw how Mother and dad had declined health-wise, and were even worse off financially than the time he had last seen them.

76

His youngest brother, ten-year-old Jim, was doing many of the chores in addition to going to school. Mother's memory was slipping and his once hale and hearty blacksmith father had aged considerably.

After a visit with the folks and a good night's rest, Joe hitched his way to the recruitment office in Des Moines. Ever with a sense of adventure, Joe wanted to pilot fighter planes, but quickly walked out of the office disappointed. He was rejected because of his color vision deficiency. Off to the Marines Recruitment Office, only to face rejection again.

By the next stop, he was feeling considerably down. When he walked in, the recruiting sergeant was sitting at his desk as the afternoon sun streamed in the window. Joe explained how he had been turned down because of his color blindness, his inability to tell the difference between red and green. Not fazed one bit, the sergeant held up a piece of yarn.

"What color is this red yarn?" the Army Air Corps recruiter asked with a hint of a smile. By evening, Joe was at Fort Des Moines doing KP duty washing dishes. It was January 15, 1942, and Joe had just turned 22.

It wasn't long before Joe got orders to head to the base in Texas for basic training. Dressed in his uniform, good-looking Joe Dew caused quite a stir among his sister Goldie's co-workers when he walked in to tell her good-bye at the Langwear factory where all were busy making parachutes for the war. Goldie had tears in her eyes as she hugged Joe. "Don't worry about anything," she said, "I'll keep my eyes on the folks and Jim. You just take care of yourself and come home safe."

As he boarded the train to Texas, Joe thought about his family and where the war would take his brother John, who had joined the army. It would be a long stretch before both he and John saw Iowa and family again. John was leaving behind his five-year-old son, Leroy, in Boone with Aunt Belle. John's ex-wife, Peggy (Violet) had taken off and left their young son with him.

Training at Sheppard Field in Texas wasn't a problem for Joe, who was used to hard physical labor. But putting up with the abominable sand was another story. As he told the story, frustration crept into his voice, "There was sand in my clothes! Sand in my eyes! Sand in the beans! Gritty, disgusting sand was everywhere!"

Mechanic Training

Joe wasn't a bit sorry to say good-bye to basic training and head to Chanute Air Field, the United States Army Air Service Technical Training Command, 130 miles south of Chicago. There Joe was assigned quarters in one of the large tents being used temporarily because of the rapid influx of servicemen. He followed orders to find the crew chief and began his training.

This particular crew chief, in charge of training crews for aircraft maintenance on bombers, was quite a character and liked by all his men. He had the distinction of being able to start his planes on cold

Illinois mornings, even when others had difficulties getting their planes going. Surprisingly, this led to quite a scandal!

According to Joe, "The crew chief was put under investigation to figure out why his planes all started so quickly when it was so cold." The chief had figured out a method to thin the cold, viscous oil. The investigation found the chief's men installed a small port on the oil lines, just before the point where the oil entered the line. Through the port a little bit of gas was allowed to flow into the line and instantly shut off. The small amount of gas added to the line thinned the oil and aided the engine in firing to life within four seconds. Then the gas quickly evaporated and caused no problems.

The investigators figured out what the chief was doing and weren't happy with him for taking it upon himself to make the modification. They abruptly demoted him to private. Joe and the crew were very upset by this turn of events. After deeper scrutiny, however, the top brass realized what the chief was doing wasn't creating any danger for the planes and was actually a safe and more effective method for starting planes in cold weather. In the end, the order came down from above to put the oil line modification on all planes. The chief got back his job and a promotion, much to the great relief of his men.

Curtiss P-40s

Finishing his training at Chanute Air Field, Joe packed his bag again. His new training assignment was P-40 Specialist School in Buffalo, New York, at the Curtiss-Wright Corporation's main facility. The sturdy Curtis P-40 was one of America's most important and sturdy fighter aircraft in World War II.

P-40s
Library of Congress

Joe was surprised to be housed in the Elks Club in downtown Buffalo. There were long rows of bunk beds with iron pipes on the legs, which enabled them to be stacked three high. It was not a quiet place. In fact, Joe saw numerous fights among the guys over who got which bunk. Reveille came at the crack of dawn, with Joe quickly jumping out of bed, dressing in coveralls, and gobbling down a hasty breakfast before lining up outside. From there, he marched in formation over a mile to the factory to work.

Elks Club
Buffalo & Erie County Public Library Research
Club Scrapbook, Vol.2. D-H, p. 115

Joe worked hard to learn the P-40 inside out. This single-seat, single-engine, all-metal war plane, at times with an identifying and menacing shark's mouth painted on its nose, and with a speed of 346 mph at 15,000 feet, flew not only for the United States but for their allies in Europe and Asia as well. The P-40 engines were not air-cooled engines, but were liquid cooled with a V8 shape. Curtiss-Wright built 11,998 P-40s before production was finally terminated in 1944.

Joe explained, "I learned how to time P-40 distributors by looking up the exhaust port at the number one cylinder. By observing the tops of the valves, I could see when the exhaust valve on the number two cylinder barely touched the bottom. That's when the number one cylinder would fire." It was a valuable technique to be able to time the distributor visually. When in the field, there would be no machines to get that job done. Before Joe left Buffalo, he mastered maintenance of the P-40. He could take apart and put together a P-40 Warhawk plane engine from one end to the other. Those skills would serve him well.

Having completed the training on P-40s, Joe boarded a train to the Orlando Army Air Base where he was assigned to maintain P-40s. As news reports came in on plane casualties, Joe thought maybe it was a good thing the Air Corps had turned him down and he wouldn't be flying planes. During the U.S. involvement in the war, 170 planes on average were lost each day between 1942 and 1945.

While in Florida keeping P-40s in top shape, Joe skipped over private first class and was quickly promoted to corporal. He enjoyed the winter in Florida, which was a far cry from icy, cold winters in Iowa. Often times, the soldiers in his tent rolled up the sides and let the warm breezes blow through while they slept on the less-than-comfortable cots. Joe spent a lot of his free time reading at the local library and researching all he could on P-40s. Saturday nights, Joe and a few of his buddies went to DeLand, Florida, to the USO dances which brought a touch of home and normalcy to their lives. It brightened the daily drudge of working to spend an evening dancing and talking with a friendly, attractive woman, as well as taking the ugly reports of the war further from their minds.

Friend Roscoe Greenup in Florida

Officer Candidate School

But Joe was destined for a different path than working on P-40 engines. Early on, the army recognized having enough officers to replace those lost in battle was going to be a challenge. In an effort to get replacements into the field as soon as possible, the army created a program to train officers at an accelerated pace. Joe was interested in this opportunity and the extra pay it would entail. As soon as it was posted, Joe signed up to take the General Classification Test.

Scoring 142 on the military test placed Joe in the "rapid learner-very superior" category. Joe did well in all areas of the test: vocabulary meaning, arithmetic reasoning, and block-counting, which assessed graphics display processing and the ability to visualize hidden sections in geometric shapes. Joe was pleased to learn he was highly qualified for Officer Candidate School. The first sergeant in his unit in Florida was also selected to participate.

Together, Joe and Sarge steamed north by train to Fort Knox, Kentucky. As the train sped through the countryside, Joe saw the first beautiful buds of spring. To pass the time on board, Sarge tried to talk Joe into heading down to the poker games. "I have to work too hard for my money to gamble it away," Joe replied curtly.

Eager to get into the game, but now thinking of the consequences, Sarge took $500 out of his pocket and handed it to Joe. "Even if I come back and ask for it, don't even think of giving that money to me," snapped Sarge as he slapped the money into Joe's hand and left the car.

Joe hid Sarge's money in his shoe, stuffed in a sock, and put it under his pillow. He climbed into the top bunk for the night as the train rumbled down the tracks. For Joe, the money he earned meant survival. He religiously sent money home, knowing the folks were struggling to make ends meet.

Officer Candidate School was a rigorous challenge, not only physically grueling but mentally demanding as well. Joe and the others took orders after orders after orders. Sarge cracked under the rigid discipline. Joe encouraged him to stay the course, but one day, Sarge had had enough. "Shove it!" he yelled at his group leader, "I don't want to be an officer that bad."

Joe worked hard and studied harder. He managed to persevere to become one of the "90-day wonders." After successfully passing the final test, Joe was given a voucher and directed to a store downtown. There he was outfitted and given his smart-looking Hart Schaffner Marx wool uniform. During the ceremony, Joe stood proud as he received his shiny second lieutenant's brass bars.

2nd Lieutenant Joe Dew

Tank Training 9th Armored Division

Joe packed his duffle bag and boarded the troop train to join the Tank Corps in Fort Riley, Kansas, ready to train with the 9th Armored Division, 19th Tank Battalion. Training was intense and included a variety of ranges. The most demanding for Joe were the night warfare exercises.

While there, Joe went to USO dances, where he met a sweetheart of a girl. They dated a number of times, but by summer, they had to say good-bye when Joe was sent to train in the harsh conditions at the desolate Desert Training Center, California-Arizona Maneuver Area (DTC-CAMA) in the Mojave Desert at Camp Ibis, near Needles, California.

There Joe and his unit trained extensively in desert survival, gunnery, and armored vehicle tactics. Traveling over 200 miles in maneuvers through 18,000 square miles of land was common. The conditions were intensely harsh. Blowing sand and extreme heat bombarded them in training exercises all the way to the Mexican border. Joe encountered brain-broiling heat during the days in the tank, and chilled-to-the-bone nights in these sizeable maneuvers which simulated the hazards of combat over extended lengths of time.

On several weekend leaves, Joe and his new buddies made the three-hour drive to Las Vegas, Nevada taking in all the sights with the ever-flashing, garish neon signs and spectacular shows. While his buddies gambled, Joe never was tempted.

Next stop was Camp Polk, Louisiana. When General Patton led war maneuvers there, he declared, "If you could take these tanks through Louisiana, you could take them through hell." The range for war exercises covered nearly two million acres of humid, swampy, and plain miserable land. Joe learned to maneuver the over thirty-ton tanks in swamps with chiggers, ticks, and mosquitoes. With 19 divisions (about 400,000 troops) engaging in mock battle, it was the largest military exercise ever held in the United States. His experiences there and an understanding of what tanks could do in swampy conditions would later save his life and the lives of him men when their tank got stuck in the mud in Germany.

Joe's final training was in Texas. At last, Joe passed the final examination and was ready to join the war effort in Europe. He boarded a bus for the journey home to see his family one last time before being shipped overseas.

When Joe saw a paint sale at a stop in Kansas City, he couldn't resist. Thinking how shabby home had looked before he had left, he purchased five gallons of white paint and arranged for them to be shipped the cheapest way to Redfield. Unfortunately, the paint arrived weeks after Joe left for Europe and his parents' place never did get painted. After a short visit with family, Joe again headed east.

"Last Stop USA" for Joe was Camp Shanks, New York. Joe, along with over a million soldiers, prepped for the war overseas from these 2,040 acres of farmland which had been hastily transformed into an army war staging area. Many were headed for the D-Day invasion and the war in Europe. Here Joe and the others spent a little over a week completing paperwork, getting shots, and making sure they were equipped for the battles to come.

Leave at Camp Shanks meant going into New York City. It was an intense and exciting place for an Iowa country boy on one last fling before life and death in Europe. Joe and his buddies boarded the train to travel nineteen miles to see the sights.

Towering skyscrapers, a multitude of people, amazing architecture! They rambled down Broadway and saw the famed New York Stock Exchange on Wall Street with its towering columns. Joe marveled at the Trinity Church Cemetery with its 1700s gravestones and fancy wrought iron fence. The son of a blacksmith, Joe appreciated how much work it had taken to make such an intricate fence.

Trinity Church fence and cemetery
Taken by James Schapiro

A stiff breeze blew as Joe and his buddies crossed to Staten Island on the ferry for five cents. The sun shone on the Statue of Liberty, her torch of freedom held high in the sky. In the evening, Joe went to a performance of the opera *La Traviata* with a high society gal he met at the USO. Afterwards, they had drinks and strolled down Fifth Avenue.

The next day, Joe went to see a matinee showing of the high-kicking Radio City Music Hall Rockettes. As they danced through the aisles, a beautiful, dark-haired Rockette sat down on good-looking Lieutenant Dew's lap and made a date for later that night. Joe left the theater in high spirits. His hopes for a date with the Rockette, however, were dashed when he got lost on the subway and didn't make his way back in time for a date.

Radio City Music Hall
Taken by James Schapiro

Returning to Camp Shanks, Joe received his "Alert" status. That meant he would be shipping out within twelve hours. Joe packed and was ready to take the train from the camp to the docks. When the soldiers arrived on the wooden pier, Red Cross Gray Ladies handed out coffee and doughnuts as the men boarded. From there, the soldiers were ferried to the waiting troopship. The men trudged onto the ship loaded down with their heavy equipment. They were on their way at last to the fighting in Europe to join what was truly a war encompassing the entire world.

Off to War in Europe

The converted passenger ship, *Aquitania*, was crowded and the rough seas caused a lot of seasickness. Fortunately, Joe managed to avoid a queasy stomach. The troopship carrying nearly 10,000 troops, along with a convoy of other ships, zigzagged its way across the Atlantic in order to avoid enemy submarines and to try to protect the ships from being torpedoed to pieces.

Aquitania

Joe had an assigned time to take his turn sleeping on the big, crowded troopship where the bunks were stacked five high. Cleaning duty, drills, and inspections filled the rest of the time. At night, beautiful luminescent waters reminded him of the forest foxfire at home. After nine days, they landed in England and stayed a while in Bath. Everyone was jittery thinking of what lay ahead.

When he wasn't in training and missing home, Joe bought an old bike and used his down time to check out the area. The quiet roads took him through the peaceful, hilly countryside. He saw small farms where sheep lazily grazed in the green fields, bringing back memories of a now-distant Iowa and home.

Joe knew once he was in battle, and it wouldn't be long, he would be able to send more home to help his folks. His father was the beneficiary of the life insurance the army made available. Joe also sent home $40 in pay and the government added $60. One hundred dollars monthly was just enough for his folks and brother Jim to make ends meet. It was the only money they had coming in except for a little egg money and the odd job his father was still able to do.

741st Separate Tank Battalion: A, B, C, D Companies

Finally, news of the June 6 D-Day invasion came! The headlines stateside read *Allied Armies Land in France in the Havre-Cherbourg Area: Great Invasion Is Underway*. The 741st Tank Battalion was part of the first wave to land on Omaha Beach, 45 men were killed and 60 wounded.

The 741st Tank Battalion initially was attached to the 1st Infantry Division to support the 16th Infantry Regimental Combat Team landings on Omaha Beach, but was attached to the 2nd Infantry Division on June 15, 1944, which it supported for most of the remainder of the war.

Several days after the D-Day landing, Joe boarded a ship late at night in England with nearly 100 on board to cross the channel to France. From the ship, the men took small boats crammed with 15 men and their gear to shore and landed in Cherbourg after midnight. There were no lights onshore, only the ominous glow of shells exploding with some even hitting the water not far from their boats. In a jeep, they drove through the perilous night with all lights turned off. Joe and another replacement officer, Lt. Victor Miller, were dropped off to join 741st C Company, about 10 miles in.

In quick order, they found the captain in charge. "Find an empty fox hole and crawl in it. I'll see you in the morning," the captain barked grumpily. It was a fitful, uncomfortable night with little sleep in the two-foot by six-foot by eighteen-inch foxhole as German artillery shells exploded in the night sky.

In the morning, Second Lieutenant Joe Dew was assigned to command a platoon in C Company, 741st Separate Tank Battalion, which was supporting the 2nd Infantry Division. Joe's assigned platoon was composed of 5 tanks and 25 men. The second in command of the platoon, the sergeant, had been put in charge after the death of the lieutenant in the landing on Omaha Beach and was relieved to see Joe. Everyone knew whoever was in the lead tank with its clearly distinguishable big radio antenna had the most chance of being fired upon first by the Germans. Officers were their prime targets. Joe calmly told him, "Don't worry, Sarge. You can relax. I'll take the lead."

The inside of their tank was claustrophobic, noisy, smelly, and exceptionally dangerous with the engine right behind tightly packed rows of ammunition. The escape hatches were especially tight to accommodate the one-by-one exit of five people (a gunner, loader, radio operator, driver, and commander) in case of an emergency.

Their path to Paris was hindered by thousands of farmers' fields. High, dense hedgerows separating the small fields were a threat. Five- to 15-foot-high dirt and rock rows, covered with thick tangles of trees and shrubs, made it difficult to see and move safely forward. These hedgerows defined the farmers' small field property lines and kept in livestock, but the narrow openings to enter the fields were mined by the Germans with booby traps. Each time a Sherman tank crawled over a hedgerow, the vulnerable underside was exposed to enemy attack, which made their movement from field to field extremely treacherous.

In order to avoid the disaster of entering the farmers' fields from mined openings and to avert exposing the tanks' undersides, the sergeant used heavy angle iron from the debris of the D-Day landing to make teeth they welded onto a beam on the front of the tank about one-and-a-half feet off the ground. Then, Joe, in the lead tank, ran into the hedgerow away from any field openings and lifted the dirt, allowing them to batter their way from one field to the next. This way, they rammed into a field anywhere they wanted and surprised the Germans, often burying them as they lay in wait.

Tank with welded teeth

Finally, after three months of relentless fighting, the 741st had battled their way to Paris, which was freed due to the courageous efforts of the Allies and the French Resistance. The French people were overjoyed after four years of German tyranny. The 741st was ordered to clean their tanks and get ready for the liberation parade through the city. August 29, Joe looked out from his tank and felt the excitement of the people as he drove with his platoon and the 28th Infantry Division down the streets of Paris.

Crowds cheered madly and pretty girls blew kisses as the tanks paraded past. It was a very moving occasion after months of intense fighting to be driving down the Champs-Elysees and around the Arc de Triomphe just four days after the Germans officially surrendered the city.

Captain Young in Paris

Joe and his men bivouacked in the evening on the outskirts of Paris. The next day, they got a break from the stress of battle to sightsee in the famous City of Lights. Joe and his buddies walked the streets of Paris and gazed in awe at the grand architecture and quaint French shops. The streets were lined with sidewalk cafés where they stopped to have a glass of wine. He visited the Louvre and marveled at incredible paintings and sculptures. His eyes grew big as this country boy saw Hermaphrodite sleeping on a marble bed. "The bed looked so soft and real that I reached out and ran my fingers over its pleated mattress and ornate tufts, but it wasn't soft at all," remembered Joe.

On to Les Invalides to see Napoleon's tomb. After having fought to free Paris, Joe was a little miffed when he took a step toward the tomb and a French guard curtly stopped him and made him take off his hat as a sign of respect for the long dead emperor. Climbing two-thirds of the way up the Eiffel Tower gave him a panoramic view of the city. Joe went from the top of Paris to the bottom, where he descended into the sewers. As he walked along the edge of the sewage, he was relieved the huge, arched tunnel had only a slight smell.

93

For a brief time, life seemed so normal, but the war was not over. All fall, Joe and his men chased Germans through Luxembourg and Belgium. The 741st Tank Battalion saw almost constant action in battle after battle.

Ending each day, Joe reported for orders. When he got back to the tanks, his men had his bedroll spread out on the hard ground accompanied occasionally with a bottle of wine, hopeful 2nd Lt. Dew, better known to his men as Skeeter, might entertain them with some tunes on his harmonica like he did when they drove back from battle. As Joe played "Goodnight, Irene," his men laughed and razzed him he didn't play nearly as well as he boasted he had back in Iowa on the Mosquito Creek where he had gotten his nickname. It was comforting to share a few moments of camaraderie and normalcy at the end of a harrowing day.

The Siegfried Line

Tension built in the descending winter as the battalion neared the German border. The Siegfried Line, better known as the dragon's teeth, stretched for more than 390 miles and had thousands of concrete pillboxes, tunnels, and tank traps located just behind the line. They were a dangerous barrier to entering Germany. The pyramid-shaped pillars were roughly three feet at the top down to six feet at the base. They were in staggered rows four feet apart to block movement into Germany.

September 14, 1944, orders came to move out. It was a day of heavy rain, near-zero visibility, and a quagmire of muddy roads. Their mission was to get through the dragon's teeth, destroy the pillboxes, and take control of the high ground. Facing three days of intense battle, Joe's platoon of five tanks fought its way to the line. The 2nd Infantry Division was unable to move forward due to heavy small arms, mortar, and artillery fire.

The weather was miserable and made the drive hard in the rugged terrain. Because of heavy rain mixed with fog limiting visibility to less than 400 yards, air support could not be used.

Dragon's Teeth southwest of Prüm, Germany

The German defense lay ahead of them and was well-engineered with their immense concrete pillboxes and mine fields. These covered pillboxes were often camouflaged with moss or made to look like straw mows. In the cover of night, engineers from the 2nd Infantry were sent to blow a path through the Siegfried Line in advance of the tanks of the 741st C Company. Sadly, the men sent by the 2nd Infantry, Lt. Whidden and three of his engineers with a satchel of demolitions, were blown to smithereens around midnight. The German's defensive line stood firm.

The next morning, the infantry received heavy small arms and automatic weapons fire from the pillboxes to the front and flanks. By 10:00 AM, the tanks arrived and Joe stopped his platoon to assess the situation. Major Yeager radioed that troops were halted by the dragon's teeth and he would have to call up another group of engineers with demolitions to attempt to blast through. Radioing back, Joe said, "I think I can break through the line, Major." Headquarters radioed back, "I don't think you can do it, Joe, but go ahead and try."

With explosions all around, Joe told his driver to pull within a few feet of a pillar. "Load an armor piercing high-explosive shell," he ordered his gunner. Because the tank was so close to the pillar, it was impossible to sight by using the periscope even with the divot fitting Joe had devised to coordinate the periscope with the gunner's sight, an accommodation which had been quickly adopted for all tanks. Joe thrust open the turret and precariously climbed out to lie on the top of the tank and line up the shot.

He then ordered his gunner, "Traverse left. Steady on." Wallace fired and shattered the concrete tooth. There was a burst of noise as dust and reinforcing rod exploded into the air. They had knocked a huge chunk of the tooth away. They continued until they used all their armor piercing ammo and the dragon's teeth lay in shatters, making a path to cross into Germany through ten yards of rubble.

After the dust cleared, Joe shouted, "Hulsey, do you think you can make it across?" He hollered back, "I will, if you say so, Lieutenant." Once through, Joe ordered the rest of his tanks to follow. His platoon, although under heavy fire, was through by 11:35 AM.

Siegfried Line
Library of Congress

He Climbed Out of Tank to Aim Big Gun

THE NEW YORK SUN

With an American Tank Battalion in Germany, Oct. 13 (Delayed) (A. P.).—Lieut. Joseph H. "Skeeter" Dew, 24-year-old tank leader from Redfield, Iowa, was recommended for decoration today for climbing out of his Sherman tank and aiming its 75-millimeter gun to breach concrete barriers of the Siegfried Line despite enemy fire from nearby pillboxes which had stopped the infantry.

His tank was only fifteen feet from a row of tooth-shaped concrete barriers guarding the western border of Germany, southwest of Prym. This was too close for his gunner, Corporal Albert A. Wallace of 2608 Avenue R, Brooklyn, N. Y., to use his sights, so Lieut. Dew, squatting on the front armor, sighted along the barrel of the 75 and gave the order to fire.

Lieut. Dew continued to sight in this manner until the shells had blown a row of four "dragon's teeth" to bits, leaving a gap through which his tank and the rest of the platoon rumbled triumphantly toward the pillboxes. In the ensuing battle, the Germans knocked out a couple of his tanks, killing two men and wounding six of the platoon. Lieut. Dew destroyed two anti-tank guns and forced another to withdraw.

"There were dead Jerries all over those pillboxes," Lieut. Dew said. "We must have fired forty or fifty rounds from our .75. We ran out of armor-piercing shells and had to use high explosive shells."

"Lieut. Dew did this voluntarily after another officer said he didn't think he could break the dragon's teeth," said Pfc. Ernest A. Arena of 6105 12th avenue, Brooklyn, a loader on Lieut. Dew's tank.

Other crew members were Woodrow W. Hulsey of Greenwood, S. C., and Pfc. Lynn Hurte of Paint Lick, Ky.

In the distance, Joe spotted a German officer and his driver racing across the field in front of them. Joe yelled at the bow gunner, "Shoot the sonofabitch! Shoot the sonofabitch!" With all the artillery fire, he couldn't hear him, so Joe drew his Colt .45 pistol and fired, but missed.

Straight ahead was a German pillbox burrowed into the earth with an opening facing toward Joe and his tanks. As they were being fired on, Joe zeroed in on the pillbox opening with the periscope and saw no big gun. "Load the phosphorous smoke shell," yelled Joe, "Fire!" When it exploded, a thick fog enveloped the pillbox and the Germans scrambled out the backside.

They were being shot at from all directions. From a group of trees a quarter of a mile away, an anti-tank cannon fired. Joe heard an explosion behind him. They backed up the tank just as another

97

round exploded, narrowly missing them. Another explosion and the track on the tank following them was knocked off.

Joe directed his gunner to traverse right and load their last high explosive shell, which hit its mark. Joe watched as the Civil War-looking cannon cartwheeled 40 feet into the air. He then climbed out of his tank to check Sarge's tank 50 feet behind them.

Sarge was just climbing out to assess the damage after the hit as per protocol. In an instant, another round hit the tank and shrapnel bounced off, hitting Sarge. Joe watched horrified as Sarge fell on the ground in a pool of blood with his guts spewing out. Joe ran to him, helpless, as Sarge weakly tried to rake them back in. For a brief moment, Joe thought, "He's going to get dead grass in his wound." But he quickly realized there was nothing he could do for him. Sarge was gone within moments and they had to move on. The medics would be there soon enough, but to no avail.

Within two hours, they secured the area. The infantry finally advanced and moved through the line. Three hours later, the tanks, out of ammo, were ordered back to be serviced, fueled, and reloaded. The Germans were pushing hard.

Moving back the next day, one of the tanks in Joe's platoon approached the same pillbox they had secured the previous day. The Germans fired and the tank was blown into the air. Regrettably, the area had to be re-secured. This time they used tank dozers to cover the pillboxes completely with dirt and render them unusable. Again, Headquarters decided to pull back.

Tired, Joe's platoon went back to camp and prepped to go again. Joe and his men were given orders to attack the Siegfried Line further on. This time, Joe's platoon wasn't in the lead. The Captain radioed the lead tank commander, "We need to get through that line. Can't you do what Skeeter did?"

"Hell no!" the leader curtly replied. However, in subsequent battles, Joe's method of blasting through the line was adopted, saving many engineers' lives.

Forward movement stopped when his platoon came to a road block. Joe pulled his tanks to the side of the road and waited in a grassy field to assess the situation. Two bloated, dead cows, a common sight, lay beside the road. He radioed his captain and was told to wait until the barricade was cleared.

Army engineers planted explosives under the tangle of barbed wire, felled trees, and land mines. According to Joe, "I saw them ignite the fuses and get the hell out of the way." The explosion cleared their path and Joe's platoon then continued on a few miles south paralleling the Siegfried Line, but made little advance. The troops picked up some ground, but were ordered to stop.

Progress was slow. The attack to push into Germany lasted nine grueling days and was one of the major stands by the Germans since Allied forces had landed at Normandy.

Maj. Gen. Robertson, Lt. Joe Dew, Col. Skaggs   Joe's DSC

In the field, Second Lieutenant Joe Dew was awarded the Distinguished Service Cross, for his "extraordinary heroism in connection with military operations against an armed enemy" for breaking through the Siegfried Line. According to the federal regulations set by Congress in 1918, in order to receive this medal, "the act or acts of heroism must have been so notable and have involved risk of life so extraordinary as to set the individual apart from his or her comrades."

Below is a transcribed letter received from the United States Army detailing the awarding of the Distinguished Service Cross to Joseph H. Dew for his heroic acts on September 15, 1944 in breaking through the Siegfried Line in Germany.

HEADQUARTERS
FIRST UNITED STATES ARMY
APO 230

GENERAL ORDERS
NO.   7   *10 January 1945*
                                                            SECTION
Award of Distinguished Service Cross------------------------------------I
Award of Bronze Star Medal--II

I—AWARD OF DISTINGUISHED SERVICE CROSS—Under the provisions of AR 600-45,22 September 1945, as amended, and pursuant to authority contained in paragraph 30, Section I, Circular 32, Headquarters European Theater of Operations, United States Army, 20 March 1944, as amended, the Distinguished-Service Cross is awarded to the following officer:

First Lieutenant Joseph H. Dew (then Second Lieutenant), 01017451, 741st Tank Battalion, United States Army, for extraordinary heroism in action against the enemy on 15 September 1944, in Germany. First Lieutenant Dew's tank platoon was supporting an infantry company and a group of engineers in reducing a defensive installation of the Siegfried Line. Intense artillery, mortar and small arms fire pinned the foot troops to the ground, preventing them from blowing a gap through the dragons teeth and retarding the advance of the tanks. Realizing that the heavy defensive fire was preventing demolition attempts by the engineers, First Lieutenant Dew, with utter disregard for his own safety, climbed from his tank turret. Standing in a completely exposed position atop his tank, he sighted along the tube of the gun, assisted his gunner in aiming the weapon and, after repeated attempts, successfully blasted a path through the dragons teeth sufficient for the passage of his tanks. Although foot troops were still unable to advance due to the intensity of the hostile fire, First Lieutenant Dew heroically led his tanks through the breech and personally directed them in destroying two anti-tank guns and forcing the withdrawal of others. The personal bravery, tenacity of purpose and conspicuous leadership displayed by First Lieutenant Dew exemplify the highest traditions of the Armed Forces. Entered military service from Iowa.

Additionally, Major General Gerow wrote a letter of commendation recognizing the entire 741st Tank Battalion for their valiant efforts and crucial role thus far in the war.

> *SUBJECT: Commendation*
>
> *TO: Commanding Officer, 741st Tank Battalion*
>
> *Upon the relief of the 741st Tank Battalion from attachment to this Corps I desire to express to you and, through you, to the officers and men of your command, my personal thanks and appreciation for the excellent manner in which they functioned while under my command.*
>
> *The 741st Tank Battalion has already been cited in orders by the First U.S. Army for the manner in which it performed the assault on the beaches of Normandy on D-Day. Since that time it was of invaluable assistance in the support of the 2nd Infantry Division in the assault on Hill 192. After the capture of this key terrain feature your battalion materially assisted in the crossing of the Vire River in the operation which led up to the capture of Vire. During the latter half of September 1944, the 741st Tank Battalion was attached to the 28th Infantry Division and supported the 110th Infantry Regiment in the initial penetration of the vaunted Siegfried line. The achievement of the battalion in shooting out the 'dragon's teeth' in this line is one of the outstanding accomplishments in the employment of tanks.*
>
> *The 741st Tank Battalion is a good, hard fighting outfit. It is battle tested. It is with regret that I accept its loss to this command. My thanks and best wishes for your continued success go with each and every one of you.*
>
> *L. T. Gerow, Major General, U.S. Army, Commanding*

Thrilled their buddy Joe had received the country's second highest medal, several officers from Joe's company wrote the newspaper in his hometown in Iowa to get a copy of the news story of Joe's heroics. The government knew the importance of letters to the troops' moral and expedited sending thousands of letters. Mail censors read, then photographed the seven-inch by nine-and-one-eighth-inch letters and shipped them as thumbnail-sized images on negative microfilm. Once stateside, the negatives were enlarged to 60 percent of their original size, printed on paper, and delivered. One hundred and fifty thousand one-page microfilmed letters in a single bag replaced 37 mailbags, thus freeing space to transport much needed war supplies.

To: Redfield Review
   Redfield, Iowa

From: 1ˢᵗ Lt. V.L. Miller
Co. C   A.P.O. 230
% pm. N. York, N. Y.
5 Nov 1944   Germany

Dear Sir:

  We the under mentioned, Capt. R.C. Young, Capt. H.E. Lippman, 1ˢᵗ Lt. G.H. Covington, 1ˢᵗ Lt. R.M. Arron, 1ˢᵗ Lt. F.L. Miller, Jr. being fellow officers in the same company and having all been present when Lt. Skeeter Dew made his famous attack on Siegfried Line, request that you send us copies of the story published in your paper concerning his courageous feat in breaking the formidable line.

  If it takes several weeks to receive said copy we still shall be looking for the article as Lt. Dew is one of our favorite stars and deserves everything that was said about him. As he has been telling us of the merits of Redfield and what a wonderful football team they had when he played for them.

  In all seriousness I sincerely hope you will grant our request as we think Joe is a darned swell fellow even though he can't play the mouth organ as well as he says.

Sincerely,
Capt. R.C. Young, Capt. H.E. Lippman
1ˢᵗ Lt. Arron Covington & V. Miller

V-Mail transcript

Schnee Eifel

All the men were feeling the stress and losses from the intense battles pushing toward Germany. A number of men were sent to the rear suffering from "combat fatigue." Equipment was failing and needed maintenance badly. Fall was turning cold and headed toward winter in this densely pine-covered terrain in the Ardennes Mountains.

October 5, the battalion pulled back to Schnee Eifel, a thickly forested mountain range called Snow Mountain by the men. Near the border of Belgium and Germany, they needed to rest, replenish supplies, and do essential maintenance on the equipment before pushing on. One battalion remained forward as a holding action in case of enemy counter-attack.

At Schonberg, Belgium, the men were quartered with families. It was the first time since his stay in England that Joe had gotten to sleep in a real bed. "The town's families made all of us men feel wonderfully welcome," recalled Joe. It was a good, though momentary, relief from the horrors of war.

Ardennes Mountains

A mile from the little hamlet in the Ardennes, the 741st Battalion quickly set to work building a base camp at the site of an abandoned lumber company where Joe's carpentry and building experience were called into service. They used a tank dozer to clear the snow-covered trees and dug out a spot for the "garrison" mess hall Joe designed. He showed the men how to make a jig for the trusses. Cement blocks were laid for a stove, using tile pipe for the chimney.

Mess Hall

Mess hall trusses

Dugout where officers slept

Tank and shed

After building the camp, which seemed like a fun diversion even with the cold, they worked on the equipment and rested for the coming encounters. At night, a trip wire was set around the camp to trigger a warning flare at the approach of the enemy. Everyone took turns standing guard. Joe recalled, "I got my first sight of Buzz Bombs at Schnee Eifel. Those one-ton warheads sizzled as they traveled through the dark night toward their targets. We held our breath as we waited for the silence signaling the bomb's motor had shut off and the bomb was falling. It was a tense time."

The Battle of the Bulge
~19,246 American dead, 62,489 wounded, 26,612 captured/missing
~1,400 British and Canadian dead, wounded, captured/missing
~10,749 German dead, 34,439 wounded, 22,487 captured/missing
~3,000 civilians dead

The equipment was finally in running order and the men were somewhat rested. Word came to move out and on December 11, the battalion rolled out of the relative calm in snowy Schnee Eifel to face the last-ditch effort of the German offensive. Eighteen inches of snow blanketed the ground with sub-zero temperatures. Even riding in the tanks did little to alleviate the cold. Heavy fog prevented air support for the Allied troops. A, B, and C platoons were sent to Robertville, Belgium, and then on to Rocherath to take defensive positions near the town. Joe was assigned two tanks to cover a forest crossroad. However, due to a faulty generator, Lieutenant Victor Miller's tank and another tank remained guarding the Ruppenvenn crossroads as Joe moved his tank to the edge of the village.

The following is a letter in Joe's own words from 1981 in response to *The Shock of War* author J. C. Doherty's request for information detailing Joe's experiences in the Battle of the Bulge.

"It was dreary, cloudy, and cold, as my platoon took defensive positions commanding views of the roads leading into Rocherath on the northeast and east. My tank and crew were backed into an

old barn having thick stone walls, facing the main road, which was approximately 300 feet away. An alley branched off this road and ran by us immediately to our left. There were thick bushes with no leaves along the road and our side of the alley.

Lieutenant Miller and his platoon were outside Rocherath a mile or more. Unfortunately, they were in the open, an undesirable position, but it's hard to hide a Sherman tank.

Lieutenant Crisler (battlefield promotion from Sergeant) was in Rocherath, southwest of my platoon.

The infantrymen in the area weren't too near, as they never liked to fight too close since we "drew fire."

It was obvious we were prepared for an attack, but just when we were apprised of it, I can't recall. It was very unusual for us to take a position such as this, for prior to this we were usually on the move attacking. It really doesn't take long to move a platoon into the best position available, provided one is near.

The old barn my tank was in was a fairly defendable position, easy for us to see out and hard for others to see in.

Flares that night turned night into day and were the first indication of enemy action. The flares appeared to come from the south and east.

The tank I was in developed generator trouble, and we couldn't use the power traverse motor for the turret. The turret had to be cranked by hand. We had to save battery energy for the starter.

There was a tank from another platoon to our southwest. I remember telling the tank commander he'd be wise to move in alongside a building before nightfall, as his tank was right out in the open. He didn't move.

Later, when it was completely dark, flares lit up the sky turning night into day. Among the first to get hit was the tank I'd tried to get to move. It sounded like 88s. They have a characteristic "wack-poo" at close range. I don't believe we fired a shot the first night, but neither did we sleep.

Next morning, we heard that the SS had captured some of our infantrymen, lined them up against the wall of a building across the street and shot them down. Our infantry knew they couldn't surrender and live…we got the message too.

About mid-morning, three tanks clanked in from the east with strange looking muzzle breaks on the gun barrels, and stopped broadside to us…in plain view, not over 300 feet away. They were German Mark Vs. My gunner used armor piercing ammunition. The first shot made a jagged hole about 18 inches across the side of the first tank.

My gunner then put one into the second and third tank in succession. They never had time to figure out where we were or to turn their guns on us. As the Germans were scrambling out of their tanks, our infantry were picking them off. At least one German tank was on fire. There was a fourth tank in line with just its gun showing that backed up out of sight and left.

The rest of the day was fairly quiet. We ate K rations that we had in the tank and tried to keep warm.

That night, after it was pitch dark, we heard a German tank clanking and creaking slowly coming down the alley directly toward us. We heard a German on foot apparently leading the tank driver in the fog. I heard him say, "Halt!" to a cow that moved in the alley and heard a short burst from his burp gun.

I told the driver to be prepared to start the engine after we had fired and to get the hell out of there. We did just that. The H.E. went off against the front of the German tank. As we moved north and then northwest, the German tank fired its big gun and blew off the east wall of the barn. Stones and concrete rained down on our tank.

We then moved about half a block, pulled alongside another building and faced the tank southeast. The German tank didn't follow. I know not why.

Later that night, we learned our infantry was going to pull back and leave us alone. The plan was to get the infantry several miles down the road behind us, and then when they were out of German artillery range, we were to pull out.

I heard Lieutenant Crisler's tank had been hit with a Molotov cocktail, but it didn't ignite. Fortunately, nothing happened the rest of the night, although we heard what we thought were Germans calling "Help!"

During the battle, I recall wrapping a bandage around the hand of one tank commander that had been hit by artillery. The flesh was cleaned down to the bone on the ends of his fingers. He wanted to know where the medics were and I told him they just weren't available. At least, I got his fingers covered so he couldn't see them. Evacuation wasn't available.

We didn't waste much time when we got the order we could move out. There were extended periods of being scared and I'm sure my body produced more adrenalin than ever before or since. That was the longest time I'd ever gone without sleep, and when we finally got to the rear we must have slept all day."

Back at camp, Joe learned the Germans had started shooting at the Command Post where the colonel was located. Generally, the top brass stayed safe behind the line, but unluckily had gotten caught by the surprise German attack. The colonel had ordered them to get Lt. Dew. "He can fix it," he declared. But according to Joe, "I never got the call. Fortunately, all at the Command Post got safely back to the line."

During the battle at Rocherath, C Company's Lieutenant Miller and his tank and crew were loaned to the 3rd Battalion. Miller was ordered to hold the crossroads at the edge of the forest at all costs. Lt. Miller took two tanks to cover the crossroads, which was near

Company Ks position and a battle ensued. The American tanks destroyed two panzers, but were themselves knocked out. Sadly, Lieutenant Miller was killed along with 2 of his men in the attack on December 17, 1944.

Had it not been for the faulty generator on Joe's tank, he and his men would have been guarding the crossroads. Joe was devastated by the death of his friend and wrote the following:

"A short time later, we passed through Rocherath again and I stopped at Lieutenant Miller's tank. He was my best friend. I opened the hatch and Lt. Vic Miller was sitting in his tank, dead."

Lt. Roy Aaron, Capt. Young, Lt. Joe Dew, Lt. Vic Miller

"There have been a few nightmares triggered by this period. Over the years, they have considerably lessened, but recall isn't difficult.

Shortly before the Rocherath period, we rejoined the 2nd Infantry Division. I recall getting a greeting from some infantryman that expressed friendly surprise that I was still alive.

110

We had worked as a team in Normandy and they were remarkable warriors. Most of the credit for stopping the Germans at Rocherath should go to them. They could have survived without us, but we couldn't have survived without them.

We weren't heroes, just scared kids!"

German Panzers knocked out by Joe in Rocherath

Joe's Bronze Star

Joe was awarded the Bronze Star for "Gallantry in Action during the Battle of the Bulge.

Following is a letter of commendation from Colonel Bishop to the 741st Tank Battalion.

For their part in the Krinkelt-Rocherath battle, the 741st Tank Battalion was awarded the Distinguished Unit Badge and Oak Leaf Cluster. The 741st destroyed 27 German tanks, 1 self-propelled gun, 2 armored cars, 2 halftracks, 2 trucks, and untold enemy personnel. They had 8 tanks destroyed (2 by their own crew when bogged down.)

Per General Orders No. 157, Headquarters Third United States Army, dated 1 July 1945, Companies A, B and C of the 741st Tank Battalion were cited for outstanding performance of duty in action during the period 17-19 December 1944 as follows:

Companies A, B and C of the 741st Tank Battalion are cited for outstanding performance of duty against the enemy from 17 to 19 December 1944. During a violent enemy counterattack in the Krinkelt-Rockerath area in Belgium, personnel inexperienced in combat such as cooks, clerks and drivers, manned deadlined tanks and with superb courage met the headlong plunge of the enemy and inflicted severe casualties upon him. With utter disregard for their personal safety, the officers and men of these three gallant companies faced devastating hostile tank, anti-tank and self-propelled artillery fire and fought on tenaciously against overwhelming enemy forces. Again and again the infuriated enemy threw armor and infantry against the dauntless defenders but for three days and nights these assaults were turned back by the unwavering fortitude of the inspired men. When it became necessary to withdraw to a more tenable defensive position, the tank men covered the withdrawal and were the last to leave the scene of battle. During the bitter three day engagement, they had destroyed twenty-seven enemy tanks, five armored vehicles, and two trucks. Their indomitable fighting spirit and unflinching devotion to duty are in keeping with the highest traditions of the armed forces.

The individuals assigned or attached to the above companies are entitled to wear the Distinguished Unit Badge and Oak Leaf Cluster to same in accordance with Section IV, paragraph 4, War Department Circular 333 dated 22 December 1943.

By order of Lt. Colonel Bishop: William E. Park, 1st Lt., 741 Tank Battalion, Adjutant (Acting)

Subsequently, the battalion then pulled back to Berg, utterly exhausted and cold. The men dug fox holes through the deep snow and slept as well as they could under the tanks for protection. Artillery barrages persisted through Christmas Eve into the morning of Christmas Day and continued on through a very long and anxious day. Joe and his crew did manage to crawl out from under the tank to grab a delicious Christmas meal of turkey and all the fixings, which they ate under the shelter of their tank. According to Joe, "I was very grateful for a "real" holiday meal. Those cooks deserved a medal for preparing it under such difficult conditions." After a rest and through the constant artillery barrages, they managed to get the equipment back in order, ready once again to return to a seemingly unending battle.

One by one, the towns in the Bulge were retaken with ferocious fighting. Joe was in his new position under cover of dark with the 23rd Infantry Regiment, ready for an attack south of Robertville. The situation became more perilous when the Germans started shooting flares into the night sky to locate the position of the tanks and fire on them. A tank near Joe blew up, and Joe jumped out of his tank and ran to help one of the injured men.

As Joe hurried toward the tank, a high explosive shell blasted on his right. Joe heard something zipping by and felt a sharp pain in his rear. No medics were around. His fingers burned as he yanked the hot shrapnel out. Years later, Joe went to the doctor for a painful bump on his hind end. The doctor dug out a sliver of shrapnel an eighth of an inch by three-quarters of an inch. A reminder of that frightening night!

The fighting had not been this fierce since the push to Paris. All were bone weary from week after week of unrelenting battle. But the surprise counter-offensive, the last German offensive of the war, was stopped. After five weeks of ferocious fighting, the Battle of the Bulge was over by January 25, 1945. The Germans were out of fuel and ammo. They turned tail and headed deeper into the motherland.

Rocherath was retaken. The Bulge straightened. The drive was on. The Allies were pushing hard and taking town after town. Regrettably, during this time, shrapnel mortally wounded Captain Young, on a foot reconnaissance near Joe's tank. Young had been there since the landing at Omaha Beach and was yet another hard friend to lose.

Captain Young and puppy

The Home Front

Back in Iowa, Joe's folks had been struggling for several years. But on February 2, 1945, a frantic thirteen-year-old Jim called long distance to get hold of Goldie in Des Moines. "Dad had a stroke and fell, Goldie! He managed to crawl all the way to the house through the snow. He can't do anything. He sure can't work at all." Jim was near tears and very upset, "Dad told me I have to quit school!" Goldie later told her sister, Arlene, "Things must be so much worse than I ever realized."

Goldie, Arlene, and Aunt Belle all wrote letters to Joe with their concerns. Even in the midst of war, they looked to Joe to figure things out. Joe worried Goldie couldn't handle it if she went home to take care of the folks. Years ago, after high school, Goldie had

had a nervous breakdown and ended up at the state hospital for a short stay. He didn't want her to have a breakdown again.

Knowing the pride his dad had about being self-sufficient, Joe did his best to light-heartedly convince him to get some help. Joe wrote home, but never hinted at the severe times he was facing in Germany. (*Joe went by Harold until he joined the army, then by Joe.*)

Over here
2/28/45

Hi there Pop,

Just got this thing to writing so I thought I'd write a line to you, see if you're in the mood to read a bit. Been thinking a little about how Mom is getting along...., she still takes care of the chickens and the cows?

I've wondered if you knew where and how that money I've been sending comes from and what it's for... the government pays the lion's share and I only give a small part... and it's all supposed to be used up in a month's time for your living expenses... don't go wandering down to the bank and put it in there, if I know you then I know you can put it to good use, buy a little furniture, a new stove for mom, maybe a refrigerator, some new clothes for her. What I'm trying to say is treat it as your own, which it really is, but <u>*spend*</u> *it. I've knocked out 5 German tanks and I know that helped our government plenty... a damn sight more than the amount you get each month. Mom probably needs someone to help her with the housekeeping, but I don't think Goldie is the one to do it, and you know she isn't if you'll stop to think for a minute. Don't you think you could find someone; a lot of people would like the idea. I hate to think of you and mom out there with no one around when Jim is off to school... with a hundred a month to spend and no strings attached you should be living like a king, and that's the way I want you to live. I get my regular salary besides that money, so there's plenty for everyone. What do you think, or are you undecided? At least sleep on this tonight and do what you think best, whatever it is, it's okay with me. I darn sure don't want you trying to save any of it for me, because it's against the law, and besides, I don't need it, okay?*

Things beginning to warm up there yet? Looks like spring is on the way over here. How did you come out on that railroad ground?

Be seeing you
Your son Harold "Huski"

Shortly thereafter, Joe wrote the following letter to his sister Goldie.

It ain't Des Moines
3/3/45

Hi Goldie,

Just finished writing to Jimmy and thought I'd worry a few more lines out of this machine. It doesn't spell too good, don't they make some that spell??

What do you think of the folks hiring a housekeeper? I've written to Pop and asked him what he thinks about it, but I'll bet he jumps over the roof.

They need someone there to cook and do a little housework, or at least that is what I've been led to believe by Arlene and Belle. I don't think you are the one to do it, so don't jump on me for suggesting it. I think I know how you feel about it. What do you think about it? Also Arlene told me she was figuring on taking Jim and mom down with her if anything happened to Pop...I definitely don't like that...there better be someone living on the home place when John and I get back, because it's home to us and about the only roots we have.

Do you think I could bother you again to get me a book on The Fundamentals of Radio or Elementary Electricity, by a fairly good author? One that wasn't written in 1900? I'd sure appreciate that.

Having good weather there? We are here, although it's turned a little colder the last day or so. Belle sent me a picture of John's little rascal, not a bad looking kid. I'll bet Belle will make a well-mannered boy out of him.

Have you been to any good shows lately? Last night I saw "Janie" and it wasn't at all bad. Not so good as some I've seen but good enough to take one's mind off less disagreeable subjects.

The girl in New York got the flowers okay, thanks a lot. She said they were a very pretty red, and got there for Valentine's Day.

I'd better close shop for I'm running out of things to say, write and tell me your troubles...they are mine too.

Love,
Brother Harold

116

Goldie worried what best to do, but it wasn't long before she put in her notice at the factory making parachutes for the war. She packed her belongings and took the bus to the homestead to look after her family. At that point, the little money coming in was from Joe sending money home. The money John was sending home went to Aunt Belle to take care of his son, Leroy. Goldie had to dip into the $393.50 she had managed to save to make ends meet.

Goldie and Mother

At home with the folks, Goldie took over the running of the homestead and looking after Jim and her parents. With the arrival of spring, she planted a garden, sold eggs, and pinched pennies. She kept everything running and prayed for an end to the war with the safe return of Joe and John. Joe was forever grateful to Goldie for the sacrifice she made to take care of the family, and he recognized what a demanding task it was.

Into Germany

Joe and his men spearheaded the 741ˢᵗ Tank Battalion, the first unit, into Germany chasing the fleeing Germans. Command gave Joe a new tank with a bigger 76 mm gun and put him in the lead. Even with worries about home and heartbreaking losses, there was a war going on and defeating the Germans was the utmost priority.

Mined roads were a common peril as they traveled through the German countryside. Boom! A mine went off under Joe's tank and sounded like a giant sledgehammer. Fortunately, no one was hurt, but they had to take time to fix the disengaged track.

Occasionally, Joe had to lead his platoon around a mined section of road. Here his good sense of direction and hunting experience proved helpful. They had to struggle through a thick forest for a quarter of a mile, pushing down trees as they went. The tank got hung up on a big tree and they really had to do some slick maneuvering to get unstuck.

Once, they liberated a case of wine and happily strapped it on the tank. Artillery hit them and they scrambled to escape the flames. Everyone got out safely. However, according to Joe, "We were madder than wet hens about losing that case of wine." Their damaged tank didn't stop them long. Joe took command of the tank following his and continued leading his unit deeper into German.

A little more than half a mile from a little town west of the Rhine River, Joe's platoon stopped to look over the terrain and spied a German camp. There was an open field to his left, timber on his right. He ordered his platoon into the open field and with all five tanks abreast headed for the town. Joe gave the order, "Open up with everything you have. Advance forward and stay even." They opened up with their 75mm's, 30 caliber bow guns, and turret machine guns, making a terrible racket. The Germans made a hasty departure and the townspeople ran out carrying white flags.

Joe's Zeiss aiming circle

As they approached the town, Joe's platoon stopped on a little knoll at the deserted German observation post. There were still coffee pots hanging over the burning camp fires. They found a variety of items including abandoned bedrolls and binoculars. Joe picked up a Zeiss aiming circle used to work out the range to targets. Years later, he made a tripod for it and used it to lay out stakes for his new home.

Across the Rhine

As the 741st rolled through Germany, there was a hint of spring and warmer weather. In the valleys, the terraced vineyards were sprouting green. The crew was getting accustomed to the 76 mm gun on the new tank Joe had been given. The gunner hollered at Joe, "Lieutenant, I see a big smokestack. Can I take a shot at it?" It was three miles away and Joe didn't think he'd be able to hit it, but nodded the go-ahead. The muzzle blast was terrific and shook the entire tank. As Joe recounted, "And darned if he didn't take the smokestack down!" Joe hoped their new 76 mm with a lot more punch would be a better match for the Germans, who had more powerful Tiger tanks with 88 mm guns.

Town after town, they pushed on with short, violent battles as they went, encountering pockets of determined SS troops. Joe's tank continued in the lead as they made their way to the Rhine River and the bridge at Remagen. As his tank led their unit into Germany, Joe tried to calm his men, who did not like being in the lead, by joking, "Don't worry guys. This means no dust for us!"

As they headed deeper into Germany, they weren't allowed on the wide autobahn Hitler had built to facilitate transport of troops and equipment. According to Joe, "That was now reserved for General Patton. Our battalion had to travel through the countryside. We went across a lot of bridges not knowing if they would support the weight of our 33-ton tank, and we dodged a lot of anti-aircraft artillery."

As Joe neared the Rhine River, the last major geographic obstacle to Allied troops moving into Germany, he saw an American tank ahead. Joe was wearing a French helmet, one he had kept with a better headset for radio communication, and was riding with his head out of the turret when he spied the roadblock ahead.

Sergeant Paul Mech from Yuma, Arizona of the 9th Armored Division alerted his crew as he saw a tank moving toward them and prepared to execute his orders to shoot at anything moving from that direction. Word had come down Germans were masquerading as Allied soldiers. Mech's gun was tracking Joe's tank and his gunner was ready to fire.

Joe saw the danger, crossed his arms, and started waving frantically and hollering, "Don't shoot! Don't shoot!" It was great luck Mech recognized Joe's voice from their days of training together stateside and yelled, "Lieutenant, I had my gun pointed at you ready to fire and just in the nick of time I realized it was you. That was a close call!" They firmly shook hands and Joe said his thanks.

120

Joe wearing French helmet painted white for winter

In early March 1945, at the top of a grassy knoll overlooking the Rhine River, Joe's platoon sat watching the show below. Soon German Stukas, dive-bombers, flew overhead trying to blow up the railroad bridge and were strafing the troops. Then bullets sounding like hail rained on their tank. Joe and his men quickly decided they had better skedaddle out of there. The 9th Armored Division managed to capture the bridge and get across the river, a major success.

The 741st advanced upstream and crossed the river on a rapidly constructed pontoon bridge near Neiderbreisig. Their battalion continued with steady progress, taking a town a day. They traveled for miles and miles with Germans shooting at them only every now and then. Droves of German soldiers were surrendering or deserting the cause. However, there were dangerous pockets of resistance that caused significant damage and casualties to the Allied troops.

Moving deeper into German territory, the view out of Joe's turret on April 13, 1945 was tranquil and serene with beautiful cherry trees covered in pink and white blossoms lining the road. His tank was loaded with men from the 2nd Infantry joking and laughing. In an instant, Joe's enjoyment of the peaceful ride was shattered by a blast from a bazooka. The shot went right through his driver's head and into the tank. Sgt. Walter Fryer was instantly killed.

Three infantrymen, who had been riding on the tank, lay splattered on the tank's front slope. The ammo stash inside the tank horrifically exploded. Joe was blasted out of the turret as the tank swerved off the road. He crashed to the ground, disoriented, and unable to hear anything. His face was red with blood streaming from both ears. The other survivors in the tank bailed out and were injured, but okay, their tank going up in flames!

The German with the bazooka immediately stepped forward from behind a tree waving a white flag in surrender. Joe staggered to his feet and barked an order to stop the soldiers converging on the German. Years later, Joe wondered why he had ever stopped the troops from going through with executing him on the spot.

Quickly piling into other tanks, Joe and his men, along with the 2nd Infantry Division, continued fighting their way into Dorstewitz. Joe couldn't hear well and was having difficulty discerning where sounds were coming from. As soon as the town was secured, Joe along with his remaining crew were sent back to the field hospital. Joe had cuts, bruises, a concussion, and perforated eardrums.

At the field hospital, Joe's men stayed for a week and then were sent to Paris for a one-month furlough. However, with a heck of a headache and constant ringing in his ears, the doctor gave Joe a shot of penicillin, two aspirin, and a Purple Heart, and sent him back to the battlefront after two weeks of rest. He took command of another tank and joined his platoon outside of Pilsen.

Joe's Purple Heart

Pilsen, Czechoslovakia

The U.S. army tanks rolled into Pilsen, Czechoslovakia, on May 6, 1945, and liberated the townspeople, who had been under the brutal control of the Nazis for six long years. According to Joe, "The people living in the town were awfully glad to see our battalion." Joe and his men were touched by the warm welcome they got. They stayed in apartments right across the street from the Skoda Gun Works, where all kinds of weapons for the German war effort had been made using the forced labor of the Czech citizens.

Tanks parked in Pilsen

Entering Pilsen

The people treated the troops with great kindness. Joe and several officers were invited into the apartment of a Czech family, who were so grateful to the American soldiers for risking their lives to secure their freedom. The first night, an exhausted Joe slept on an amazingly soft featherbed. When he found out the gracious family had given up their bed, he moved to the living room and slept on the floor for the rest of the week.

While in Pilsen, Joe took a jeep over to the east side of town and enjoyed strong Vodka with some Russian troops. He and his men had great respect for the Russian soldiers. They had been through tremendous fighting and deprivation. Scroungy, dirty, crooked and missing teeth, but very friendly to Joe and his buddies, these soldiers had suffered terrifically throughout the war. Around eleven million Russian soldiers died during the conflicts, along with an estimated between ten and twenty million Russian civilian casualties.

After a week in Pilsen, the commander ordered the battalion into the countryside. Joe and his men set up their tents in open farm country. Daily, the people in a nearby village came out to work in the fields. The geese waddled in a row leading the workers to their fields. It was an idyllic sight for Joe. The strong women pitched hay onto wagons pulled by oxen. At night, the geese would again take the lead, but now heading back to the picturesque village.

May 8, 1945, Victory in Europe Day came and went. There had been a number of times Joe and the others thought the war had ended only to be disappointed. Thankfully, this time it was real.

Soldiers calculated their points to determine if they would be sent home or would have to join the war effort against Japan. Points were given for length of service, service in combat, designated medals, and number of children at home. Joe hoped he had at least 85 points so he could be rotated back to the U.S. Less than that and he faced the possibility of being shipped to war in the Pacific to fight in the ongoing battle against Japan.

Luckily, Joe had enough points to linger awhile before heading back to the U.S. He and his platoon took their leave and headed by train to Switzerland. It was most assuredly a welcome leave. The mountains were breathtakingly beautiful. They rode a ski lift across a craggy canyon and saw mile-high lakes in the Alps. One of the places they stopped at was Chillon Castle in Montreux on Lake Geneva. When they stopped to look at the castle, they were pleased to be invited in for a visit.

Chillon Castle

Castle toilet

Memorable to Joe was a toilet on the top floor of the castle with two holes where he could look through to see the lake waves lapping the shore far below! Most impressive was being invited to dine with royalty in the grand dining hall. Joe sat at the long head table, which was set in style with elegant cloth napkins and more silverware at each plate than he had ever seen. The enlisted men were confused as to where to start and kept looking to Joe to see what he was going to do. He guessed correctly and started by dipping his fingers in the small finger bowl, followed by his men. It was a delicious meal and thoroughly enjoyed by all. Joe reminisced, "The entire trip was a real thrill!"

Back in Czechoslovakia, Joe was assigned as commander of an artillery unit for a week. They promoted him to captain, but he did not find out about the promotion until he was back in the States. He had not asked for it, but was pleased the higher-ups thought he had it coming. According to Joe, "It sure meant a lot later on to be able to have 'Captain' on my resume."

Joe in Czechoslovakia

After a short time as commander, Joe received orders to travel by jeep to France and arrange accommodations for the troops that followed. He rode in an advance party all the way from Czechoslovakia to dockside in Le Havre, France. On November 4, 1945, he boarded the U.S.S. *Lejeune* with over 4,000 soldiers headed home, destination the United States of America. "This sure is no luxury liner," Joe commented to a fellow soldier, "but at least we don't have to worry about German subs." After a week of sea travel, the ship was greeted by the Statue of Liberty. Joe called out, "Lady, if you ever see me again, you'll have to turn your head."

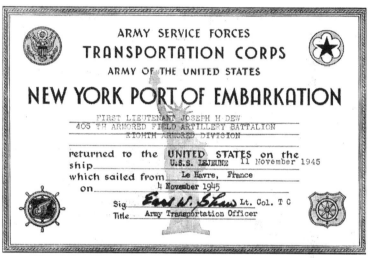

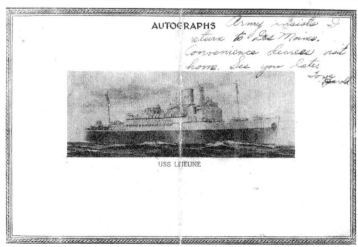

USS LEJEUNE

They landed in New York City and Joe was officially discharged from the army January 25, 1946. Like millions of men coming home from the war, Joe, 26, was more than ready to get on with his life. He bought a $110 engagement ring while in the Big Apple, planning he would settle down as soon as possible. He boarded the train and made the journey home to Iowa.

Joe's older brother John had arrived stateside six months before Joe on June 28, 1945. He too was ready to settle down to a life of normalcy, far from the horrors of war. During the war, John had asked his oldest sister Goldie to find someone to write to him. That someone was Edith Read, who worked as a domestic in Des Moines. After arriving home on a brief leave, John and Edith married and honeymooned in Chicago before he returned to active duty in Texas. His son, Leroy, continued to go to school and live in Boone with Aunt Belle. After the war ended, John started farming, but to make ends meet got a job in Adel, Iowa at the Sioux City Brick and Tile Company. Goldie was greatly relieved to have both her brothers home from war.

John, Edith, Leroy on wedding day

Back in the U.S.A

WWII Collection of the New-York Historical Society

Home at Last

Although overjoyed to be home, it was a sad homecoming for Joe. When he walked through the door, his mother had no idea who he was and his father sat in his rocking chair looking weak and sickly. He was comforted to be home, but Joe was very worried about his parents.

He found eight and a half acres across the road from the homestead for sale and bought the property with money he had saved from his time in the military. It was a triangular piece of land between the Raccoon River and the Milwaukee, Chicago, and St. Paul railroad tracks. By spring, he and Jim were building a concrete block, twelve-foot by sixteen-foot bachelor's quarters with an indoor bathroom. It had a kerosene stove for heat and bottled gas for cooking. Outside were a pretty good-sized henhouse and a little barn. Joe and Jim fenced in the small alfalfa field. Together, they dug a shallow well by hand and used fifteen-inch clay tile to line it.

Adjusting to life as a civilian and dealing with the shocks of war took some doing. Helping on the homestead and building a place nearby kept him occupied and it wasn't long before Joe decided to check out the Saturday night dance in Stuart. He enjoyed talking more than he did spending time on the dance floor, but he was a good dancer and hoped to meet someone special.

That someone turned out to be Evelyn Johnston. She had loved dances since she was a child on the farm and would rather dance than anything else in the world. When the neighborhood dance was held at their country home, her parents removed the furniture from the parlor and dining room and waxed the floors, ready for lots of fun. Since age 16, she had been going to Stuart for the dances with her older brother Willis.

However, after her father read the book, *From the Ballroom to Hell*, he would not allow young Evelyn to go. She was utterly devastated. Fortunately, after several weeks, her mother intervened and she was allowed back on the dance floor.

By the time Evelyn was 19, the United States had entered WWII. She and Willis still lived on the farm with their folks. Willis signed up for the draft, but farmers were considered essential to providing food for the war effort and were exempt. "Food Will Win the War and Write the Peace" was the slogan in the Corn Belt. Evelyn had a job candling eggs to check for freshness before they were packaged and sold. But what she most looked forward to were the Stuart dances every Saturday night.

At age 77 in 1942, Evelyn's father retired from farming and turned the operation over to his son Willis. Evelyn then moved with her mother and father to a small house in Stuart. Cleaning the outhouse there was a necessary chore. In the spring of 1944 when Evelyn was 22 and still living at home, her father contracted typhoid fever after completing this odious task. Antibiotic treatment for typhoid fever didn't begin until after the war, and sadly he died. Being the youngest of thirteen children, Evelyn was very close to her father and mother and she was devastated by his loss.

It was two years later at the Stuart dance Evelyn met Joe in February 1946. As the jitterbug was playing, Evelyn and Willis dipped and swirled across the floor. All of a sudden, Willis dropped her as she went sliding between his legs. According to Evelyn, "There I lay flat on my back in the center of the dance floor, in front of God and everybody." After a good laugh, she jumped up and they enthusiastically finished the dance.

After her misstep, Evelyn took a break from dancing. On the sidelines, she stuck her head around one of the big support posts looking for the good-looking new guy she had spied while flat on her back. She had graduated from Redfield High School two years after Joe, but had never actually met him.

Ever vivacious with flashing eyes and a great smile, Evelyn and Joe quickly struck up a conversation, and then they danced. Later, he asked her for a date the following Wednesday. By the end of the evening, she told her sister, "Gee, he was so tall and handsome and could he dance!" She was smitten.

However, on Tuesday, the mail arrived and there was a letter from Joe. He wrote he couldn't come for the Wednesday date, but he would see her "anon." Disappointed, country girl Evelyn figured it was his polite way of saying he had thought better of asking her out and she would never see him again.

It took three weeks for Joe's 1940 Studebaker to get fixed before he could again go to the Saturday night dance. Joe headed for

Evelyn's home and found her in bed with the flu. He arrived with a bouquet of red roses and an apology that his car had broken down and it had taken longer than he expected to get the necessary part to fix it. They started dating, and by April Joe was sure Evelyn was the one.

A New Beginning

They married on a beautiful spring day, Sunday, April 21, 1946 at the Boone Methodist Church. Joe's friend Ray Cummins and his girlfriend stood up with them. White, fragrant Easter lilies and lavender lilacs decorated the church alter. Evelyn was beaming in a gray wool suit with a pink flower-trimmed hat. Pink sweetheart roses surrounded the gardenia corsage Joe got her. After the ceremony, they all drove into Des Moines for dinner. At home, Joe swooped Evelyn into his arms and carried her across the threshold to begin their lives on their little farm in Redfield.

MARION STREET METHODIST CHURCH
Boone, Iowa

No honeymoon for Joe and Evelyn, but plenty of optimism as they settled in their new home. They bought two pigs, several calves, and 500 white baby chicks good for both meat and laying eggs when grown. On one chilly spring night, Joe stoked the fire in the brooder house stove and returned to the warm house for a few minutes where he accidentally fell asleep. When he awoke and went out to check on the baby chicks an hour later, 250 of them had smothered. Groundhogs, rabbits and a flood wiped out the garden. Significant losses!

Joe also bought a registered purebred, pregnant Guernsey named Buttercup. They had high hopes of having milk and a calf to sell. Buttercup had been with a herd and was very lonely on the small Dew homestead. Each night, she settled next to their little home and slept. There were two French windows that opened inward and Evelyn fretted Buttercup would back up to the window and relieve herself into her clean house on those hot summer nights.

Early in the summer, a very pregnant Buttercup got out of the paddock and newly pregnant Evelyn frantically chased her down the railroad tracks. That was money running away! Evelyn lost her footing and smashed into the tracks. Fortunately, she was okay, but unfortunately, Buttercup aborted a deformed calf. Joe's luck was not going well on his small acreage. Their hopes for making a living on their little farm continued to dim.

In truth, Joe's farming endeavors were a dismal failure. He had to get a job as a mechanic working for Lamb's Garage in Redfield for $35 a week, and also took a part-time job at the saw mill in Adel to support his new bride and the baby they were now expecting.

Sadness and Joy

Joe often went to check in at the homestead and help his folks and Goldie. Through the summer, his father did little but slowly rock on the front porch and stare into the distance. Regrettably, there was nothing Dr. Peace could do for his father's declining health. On a cool fall day, October 5, 1946, Joseph Locke Dew quietly passed away at the age of 67, with burial two days later at the East Linn Cemetery. It had been less than nine months since Joe's arrival home from the war.

Joe's mother did not even realize when her husband of 39 years died. Her dementia continued in a downward spiral and her behavior became more and more difficult to handle. Joe knew the time was coming when Goldie and Jim would no longer be able to care for her. Joe struggled, but knew he would be the one to make the difficult decision. It was a sad day when he and Jim loaded his dear, sweet mother in the Studebaker and drove her 100 miles to leave her at the Clarinda State Mental Hospital two days after Christmas.

Clarinda State Hospital for the Insane
asylumprojects.org

Shortly thereafter on the iciest, coldest day of the winter, Evelyn went into labor. According to Evelyn, "It was a still, cloudless, moonlit night with the temperature standing at twelve degrees below zero. About 8 PM, Joe went out praying our old, 1940 Studebaker would start while I packed a bag. The roads were pure sheet ice and Joe slipped off the road and skidded up an embankment. It was a long, treacherous, 20-mile ride to the small, three-bed hospital sitting in the middle of an Iowa cornfield."

As Joe recalled, "All day long, nothing happened. In the evening, the doctor sent me home to feed the animals and milk the cow, a decision I regretted when I later learned the doctor was not the best. He most certainly shouldn't have had a license to practice medicine. Fortunately, Dr. Peace, our family doctor, never left the little hospital and kept a watchful eye on Evelyn all through the night."

Evelyn remembered, "I was totally exhausted. Elaine finally arrived near noon. I can still picture Joe as he came strutting into the room carrying our little baby nestled in his arms. I looked down into a wrinkled, red, little face with long, thick black hair on her head. From that day on, she was our "Dolly.""

Evelyn and Elaine

The great joy of their newborn daughter was followed by Joe's mother's death. It had been only a few weeks since Joe and Jim had taken her to the Clarinda State Hospital. Her death certificate stated she died of "arteriosclerosis, other psychosis, and cerebral arteriosclerosis." Joe, however, always believed the staff had overmedicated her, causing her death at the young age of 59.

He felt tremendously guilty over the loss, but there was nothing to be done. It was a lesson the war had taught him. They buried his beloved mother beside his father at the East Linn Cemetery in Redfield, Iowa.

At the homestead, Goldie prepared to move back to Des Moines. She sold off all the chickens. Of the $71 she got, she had to pay Dr. Peace $51. The remaining $20 she gave to Jim, who planned to join the service. Joe figured out the finances and sold the property and anything of value, something that pained him greatly. He had sent home $1,010 for his family's support during the war and the government had added $1,890 from September 1943 to January 1946. The home and family Joe had so looked forward to returning to while overseas was gone.

Funeral expenses for JL Dew	$325		
Funeral expenses for EM Dew	$300		
Tombstones	$125		
Repay Old Age Assistance Lien	$280	Home sale	$1275
Joe's car/tools Dad had sold	$400	Insurance	$ 500
	- $1430		+ $1775

By February, Joe had sorted out and paid for all obligations. Young Jim finalized his plans to join the Air Force and Goldie packed to move back to Des Moines. On the last day of February, Goldie was ready for Joe to drive her to Des Moines. As she walked to the car carrying her bag, she slipped on the ice and badly broke her ankle. There was no choice but to move into the tiny home with Joe and Evelyn and the new baby until she recovered.

Goldie and Elaine

Figuring out their own finances, Joe and Evelyn had no illusions about farming providing the money they needed. Joe simply lacked the skills and, more importantly, the interest in taking the risks necessary to make a living at farming. He knew this wasn't the life he wanted for his new family. They had a long discussion and concluded he needed to do something different. He decided to take advantage of the GI Bill and finish his college degree at Iowa State in Ames. Goldie stayed with Evelyn and Elaine while her broken ankle mended and Joe quickly registered and began classes in March, coming home on weekends.

The Servicemen's Readjustment Act of 1944, better known as the GI Bill, had been controversial. Many believed it was a waste to spend money to send battle-weary war veterans to college. College was something typically reserved for the rich, and many believed so many returning war veterans would certainly lower standards in colleges. In 1947, Joe was one of the forty-nine percent of college entrants who were veterans. Over 7.8 million World War II veterans took advantage of either the education or training programs offered through the bill. According to the final GI Bill passed by Congress, "Our servicemen and women have been compelled to make greater economic sacrifice and every other kind of sacrifice than the rest of us, and are entitled to definite action to help take care of their special problems."

In addition to the credits Joe had earned prior to leaving for the war, the college gave him a number of credits for his life experiences: six credits for World War II military service, six elective credits, and six quarters of physical education credits. It was a great help the GI Bill provided a small stipend and paid for tuition and books. As Joe recalled, "I was very grateful for the opportunities that the bill provided."

By June, Joe and Evelyn had sold their small farm and moved to 771 Pammel Court married student housing at Iowa State. The college had hastily obtained no longer needed Quonset huts, trailers, demountable houses, and metal barracks from federal government war production sites to provide basic living quarters for soldiers. Joe and Evelyn's residence had concrete floors and housed two families, one on each end. Public laundries were shared by the families. While appreciative of having quarters on campus, Joe and Evelyn found winters in the metal units especially chilly.

Pammel Court

By the time Joe and Evelyn moved into their new home, Goldie was able to move into a small apartment in Des Moines with her old friend, Sylvia. Although she missed her time with little Elaine, she was relieved to be on her own once again. She looked around and found a job downtown at Lifetime Photo. She visited with Joe and family often and happily babysat Elaine so Joe and Evelyn could go out every once in a while.

To get around campus, Joe bought a used bicycle. He crafted a basket with holes to slip Elaine in so he could take her with him when he ran errands. Both he and Evelyn found jobs on campus, Evelyn working at the herbarium, mounting plant specimens for future study, and Joe working at the college library. They bought a brand new blue Chevrolet half-ton pickup with the money they got from selling their home and land. Joe built a rack for the pickup and used it to make extra money hauling anything he could.

Evelyn and Elaine

Joe and Elaine

More mature and focused this time around, it was a proud day when Joe graduated with his Bachelor of Science degree March 17, 1950. He earned a major in industrial economics and had minors in electrical engineering and psychology.

At a recruitment held on-campus near the end of the quarter, he met with Kenneth A. Meade, who had come from Michigan to do interviews for positions with General Motors. Joe was elated when

Meade told him that it looked good for him to get the job. Unfortunately, Joe never heard back.

Alaska Bound

Determined to make a future for his family, Joe decided to head to Alaska and take a job as an airplane mechanic with the Civil Aeronautics Authority in Anchorage. Any job was better than no job. He built a top for the pickup truck for their belongings and threw in a mattress to sleep on for the more than 3,000-mile trip north. Excited for their new adventure, they packed up and left March 19, 1950.

Evelyn and Joe

All went well through Iowa and across Minnesota, until they got to South Dakota, where they ran into a terrible spring blizzard. According to Evelyn, "It was Joe's skill and determination as a driver that got us through the slippery, snowy roads." For the most part, they camped along the highway, stopping only once at a cabin for a bath. A cold-water bath at that!

As they traveled the rough Alcan Highway, which was hastily built through the wilderness in 1942 by the United States in collaboration with Canada as an emergency supply route for the war effort, they were fascinated by the number of wild animals they saw. There were massive moose, antlered elk, snowy white mountain goats, plentiful deer, colorful ducks, soaring hawks, and king-sized mosquitoes. It was the first time Evelyn had ever been out of the state of Iowa and she was awed by the natural wonder.

One morning, Joe spied a flock of Canada geese approaching. The family was getting tired of pork and beans, so he stopped the truck, grabbed his gun, and shot one for dinner. He took the thermos and started across the boggy ground to get the goose, leaving Evelyn, Elaine, and his gun in the pickup. As he headed back, he was dismayed to see a Highway Patrol car pull up. Evelyn quickly whispered to three-year-old Elaine not to say a word. Joe didn't miss a step as he dropped the goose in the tall grass.

When he got back to the pickup, he held up the thermos and nonchalantly told the officer he was hunting for water and a place to fix dinner. The officer recommended a spot a mile down the road. Sure enough, the officer later returned to see if they were cooking goose. There was a $500 fine for shooting within a mile of the highway. Once again, they ate cold beans and enjoyed the spectacular scenery.

Elaine and Evelyn

Elaine and Joe eating beans

Their springtime journey on the gravel Alcan Highway was a jarring ordeal of mud and potholes. With bridges out or lacking, they had to ford rushing streams and navigate washed out sections of the so-called highway. The road went up and down mountains with dizzying drops. Miles from nowhere in the Yukon Territory, three-year-old Elaine developed a 104-degree fever. They bundled her under the down puff, gave her some aspirin, and let her sleep. Fortunately, she improved. Regrettably, however, Evelyn suffered a miscarriage as they made their way to Anchorage.

When they finally arrived after their exhausting journey, they found a booming community nestled among six different mountain ranges. In 1940, Anchorage's population had been just 3,000 and had jumped to a bustling 30,000 because of Alaska's strategic military importance in World War II and the subsequent growth of military bases.

As a result of the rapid expansion occurring during the war, housing was scarce. They found an old log cabin to rent with an "outhouse" attached at the end of a long-covered hallway. They felt fortunate, as next door, a family that moved in a week later was living in a tent.

They filed a claim under the Homestead Act on a parcel of land along picturesque Little Rabbit Creek. Being a veteran, Joe could move to the head of the line and was also able to use a portion of his military service to substitute for some of the five-year requirement of living on the land. They signed the papers for a building site outside of town on the edge of the wilderness and made plans to get a house built before winter set in.

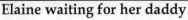
Elaine waiting for her daddy

Joe had an opportunity to take a job on the islands off the coast of Alaska, where the really big money was to be made. But as much as he valued the security money brought, he would not leave Evelyn and Elaine alone to pursue a job where he would be gone from home for long stretches.

Evelyn was decidedly unhappy in Alaska. She missed her family and Elaine kept asking to see her Aunt Goldie and Grandma

144

Johnson. They definitely didn't like the cool Alaskan temperatures going down to freezing at night. In the coming long, dark Alaskan winter, temperatures would be in the single digits and below. A typhoid epidemic among children added to the concerns of being in distant Alaska and was especially worrisome to Evelyn.

Back in Iowa, Dorothy DeFord, a worker at the post office in Redfield, received a postcard for Joe from General Motors and forwarded it to Joe's sister Goldie, who was now working in Des Moines. There had been a delay in offering Joe a job because the interviewer from GM had had a heart attack and died shortly after talking with him on the college campus.

Joe and Evelyn were ecstatic when they finally received the delayed postcard. Joe promptly gave his notice and they packed their belongings for the Lower 48. May 5, 1950, they began the grueling twelve-day journey back home to Iowa after only a few months in Alaska. On the way back, they had 21 flat tires, nearly ran out of patches, and had to buy one new tire. It was an exhausting journey, but they arrived safely back in Iowa without any serious mishaps.

Joe's Years at General Motors

Joe Dew 1950

A Move to Michigan

After brief visits with family in Iowa, Joe, Evelyn, and Elaine headed to Detroit, Michigan, with all their worldly belongings packed in the pickup. At the General Motors meeting, they gave Joe his choice of working in Detroit, Bay City, or Flint. Detroit quickly was marked off the list, because as Joe said, "The traffic in the big city was terrible." With a population of 1.85 million, Detroit was six times bigger than Des Moines. The foundries in Bay City smelled awful. Joe grumbled, "I'd rather stick with raising stinky chickens than work in the foundry there."

They decided to settle in Flint, and quickly bought a two-story house at 1309 W. Atherton, not far from the General Motors General Assembly Plant. Through the GI Bill, the government provided them a low-interest Veterans Administration home loan and guaranty. With a new job paying $315 per week for the first three months, Joe and Evelyn happily started this new chapter in their lives.

1309 W. Atherton Flint, Michigan

With a fresh start, they settled into a routine with Joe working and Evelyn taking care of the home. They spent long hours working together to convert the upstairs of their new home into an

148

apartment to help pay the mortgage. Much to Evelyn's dismay, working on the conversion often meant they were so busy they weren't able to take much time to cultivate new friendships. Once the project was completed, they rented the finished upstairs to a mother and her grown daughter from Kentucky.

With the upstairs bedrooms of the house transformed into an apartment, the downstairs had only one bedroom. At bedtime, Elaine snuggled on a foldaway cot in the dining room where she could look through the window to see the twinkling stars. She made friends in the neighborhood, mostly boys, climbed trees, played on the swing and trapeze set Joe built, and enjoyed the family's frequent fishing trips. By age five, Elaine knew the neighborhood well, had good friends, and in the fall made the mile walk all on her own to the McKinley School to start Kindergarten.

Floyd and Elaine   **Outfits sewn by Evelyn for Elaine**

Joe and Evelyn soon discovered the natural wonders of Michigan's beautiful Upper Peninsula and Canada, where they spent many weekends camping and fishing to get away from the suffocation of the city. Evelyn enrolled Elaine in toe, tap, and ballet lessons, but Elaine loved the out-of-doors more and disappointed her mother further by not wanting to play with dolls. She preferred taking her BB gun to go walking in the woods "hunting" with her

149

father. Fishing was Joe's passion. He crafted a sturdy rowboat he used to take family and friends out fishing. He even took Grandma Johnson, Evelyn's mom, out to catch sunfish on her first visit to Michigan, much to her delight.

Canadian fishing and camping

Joe and Evelyn in rowboat Joe made

Factory Life

At work, Joe quickly made friends with Harry Kaufman, who had graduated from Kansas State University, and Jim Anderson from prestigious MIT. Joe and Evelyn enjoyed playing bridge with Harry and his wife. Jim, a single man, lavished gifts on little Elaine that were not always to Joe and Evelyn's liking. However, Elaine loved to pound on the drum set and hug the fluffy, mischievous white bunny Jim got for her.

Working at General Motors was definitely a unique experience. After three months as a trainee, Joe was promoted to foreman of the cylinder head line in Plant 6. When there was a problem with the equipment, Joe dove in to figure out a solution. One day as Joe was peering into the press with his tie dangling down; the general foreman grabbed some scissors and marched over to him. Without a word, he snatched Joe's tie and cut it off. "That's a good way to lose your head," he bellowed over the noise in the shop. From that point on, Joe only wore bow ties only to work.

Heat Treat Foreman

World affairs had an impact on Joe's work soon after he began at General Motors. Unresolved conflicts over Korea at the end of World War II led to the division of Korea along the 38th parallel. Worried communism would expand when North Korea attacked South Korea in 1950, the United States became embroiled in the conflict along with other United Nations countries. The General Motors factories had contributed so much during World War II and were again called upon to make U.S. military aircraft parts. This effort hit close to home for Joe, as his younger brother, Jim, was sent to fight in Korea during the war's three-year duration.

Joe signed up for a training course for the Heat Treat Department, hoping to be able to transfer to the Metallurgical Division. His experience in the blacksmith shop, his mechanic experience working on Curtiss-Wright aircraft, and the completed course training helped him get the job in Plant 2A. According to Joe, this new position required fast-paced problem solving and quick thinking. The opportunity to be creative and use a lot of his ideas was the part of the job he found most rewarding.

The Metallurgical Division was responsible for making quality parts which had to go through a complicated heating process. The heat treatment processing of steel was able to increase its strength, hardness, toughness, ductility, or maximize its corrosion resistance, depending on the specifications demanded by each job. Parts were

151

heated in a furnace and then put in a quenching solution to cool and harden. It was a step that varied but was key in obtaining the needed end product. Depending on how the process was done with longer heating or slower cooling, the metal took on a variety of characteristics necessary for a particular part.

Joe's attention focused on the 15-inch internal gears for the Curtiss-Wright planes mass-produced from a special steel and shaped so they could be bolted on. As part of the process, the teeth were machine cut and then plated with bronze to prevent the nitrogen from penetrating them. The gears were then placed in the large nitriding furnace. Plant 2A became a very hot place to work as the heavy, circular, six-foot round lid clanged shut on the furnace, filled with nitrogen, and heated the gears to an extreme 1,000 degrees. In this process, the nascent nitrogen penetrated the steel gear body and made it exceptionally hard and wear resistant, and reduced the risk of distortion in the gear. The thinner teeth needed a different hardness than the gear body, which was accomplished by the bronze plating.

Even with this process, large quantities of the gears ended up being thrown away. The protective bronze plating did not always stick to the teeth, allowing the nitrogen to penetrate, which in turn caused the teeth to become brittle and more easily broken. Joe hated to see the waste and tried to figure out a solution.

In the lab, he experimented and mixed tin dust with kaolin---a fine clay dust imported from China---added water, and dabbed it on the surface of the steel teeth, letting it dry before putting the gear in the nitriding furnace. Eureka! He found the solution! Even better, this process was much less expensive than plating the gears with bonze. Joe was delighted at figuring out a process that saved gears, time, and money.

Plant 2A also manufactured radial engine master rods and connecting rods for the aircraft. The bearings of the connecting rods were treated with nitrogen in the furnace to form an extremely hardened surface. As the furnace's spark plug energized, it turned nitrogen into nascent nitrogen, the only form of nitrogen to penetrate the steel. However, in order to prevent the furnace's spark plug from being ruined during the process, it had to be coated with platinum, a sizeable expense.

Joe had a bright idea he could solve this problem by using a spark plug with carbon as one of the elements instead of the platinum. He figured the carbon would burn and stay fresh, instead of allowing the spark plug to become coated, which gradually destroyed the plug. At home, he pondered what to do and finally came up with a possible solution. He dismantled a flashlight battery and took out the carbon core center. He took it to the plant, drilled a hole in the end of the carbon rod, and put a screw into the carbon core electrode. He put it in the furnace, and with a big smile on his face reported, "By God, it worked!" They could use the spark plugs with carbon rather than the expensive spark plugs coated with platinum. The resulting patent Joe wrote saved General Motors a tremendous amount, and they were able to sell it to other companies. According to Joe, "I didn't get any money for my idea, but I sure did make a name for myself!"

Leaving General Motors

As much as Joe enjoyed his new position, Evelyn didn't enjoy living in Flint one bit. She hadn't made many friends and sorely missed her family. Elaine, again, was constantly asking for her Aunt Goldie and Grandma Johnson in Iowa. Only once a year, Joe's oldest sister, Goldie, was able to make the long, sixteen-hour train ride to Michigan to visit. Being twelve years older than Joe and never married, she was like a grandmother to Elaine. Joe and Evelyn took yearly trips back home to visit family, but Evelyn's mother had only been able to come to Michigan once.

Then on January 22, 1953, just two and a half years after they had moved to Flint, Evelyn's mother had a stroke and died suddenly at the age of 73. As the youngest of thirteen, Evelyn was very close to her mother, and her grief was almost more than she could bear. She tried to convince Joe to move back to Iowa, but to no avail.

Not long after her mother's passing in the summer of 1953, one of the deadliest tornadoes in the history of the country devastated the community and made Evelyn even more resolved she didn't want to live in Flint, Michigan. A severe weather bulletin was issued an hour before an F5 tornado with 261 to 318 mph winds cut a path 27 miles long in the Flint area, just 15 minutes north of where they lived. One hundred and sixteen people were killed, along with 844 who were injured. Three hundred and forty homes and 66 businesses were leveled while more than 150 more suffered significant damage, with total losses estimated at about $19 million (about $158 million in 2018 dollars). It was a jarring sight for Joe, Evelyn, and Elaine when they drove around the area a week after the tornado had gone through.

At General Motors, Joe slowly became more discontented, even though he did appreciate the creative parts of his job. He became frustrated with the whining, politicking, complaints from above and complaints from below, and working in dirty, noisy factory conditions. When his car window was smashed in the company parking lot, it was the final straw. Joe at last agreed with Evelyn they no longer wanted to live in treeless, heartless Flint, Michigan so far from family.

Evelyn had both a feeling of distress and relief on Friday, October 15, 1954, when Joe came home and told her he had marched into his boss's office and quit his job. They took a quick trip back to Iowa to discuss options with Willis, Evelyn's favorite brother. They were anxious to move back and be home, be with family. After talking things over, Willis readily agreed he would let Elaine stay with his family on the farm and send her to school while they looked for a job. Joe and family headed back to Flint and in a whirlwind of activity, put the house up for sale on Wednesday, October 20, and sold it five days later on Monday, October 25. They sold all their furniture and packed, ready to move out just a few weeks after quitting.

On Tuesday, November 2, they were ready to set off on their trip back to Iowa. Unfortunately, seven-year-old Elaine woke with very swollen cheeks and a high fever. It was a bad case of the mumps. Since Joe and Evelyn had to be out of the house for the new owners and Willis's children had never been exposed, they made a detour to Indiana and stayed with the parents of Joe's high school friend, Lavern Sloan. It took ten days before Elaine was better and they could continue their journey back to Iowa.

Once in Iowa, Joe found a job opening at Solar Aircraft Company in Des Moines, a business with over 1,100 employees. The company produced aircraft parts and had significantly contributed to making parts during the war. In the interview, the head of the company asked Joe, "What salary were you making at General Motors?" When Joe told him, he replied with a shocked look on his face, "By, God, that's more than even I make as boss of this company! You'd have better luck in California where salaries are higher." With all other options explored, reluctantly, Joe and Evelyn left a crying Elaine with her Uncle Willis and his family on the farm and headed to California to seek more lucrative opportunities.

Joe was offered several jobs in California, but turned them all down. Regretfully, Joe realized as much as he didn't like the politics and environment in the GM factory setting, the pay and benefits were the best he would likely get anywhere. The drive from Michigan to Iowa, while over nine hours, was much less than the drive from California to Iowa. As they packed once again,

Evelyn tried to raise Joe's spirits by joking maybe Michigan did have more trees than they realized.

Back to Michigan

Hat in hand, Joe headed back to Michigan with his family to see if he could get his job back. "I didn't get down on my hands and knees to beg for my job back, but it was pretty close to it," remembered Joe. Thankfully, the plant manager valued Joe's skills and put him back on the payroll at the Framing and Stamping Plant as an automation engineer.

Back in Flint by spring, the family was without a home. They rented a tiny motel room on busy Fenton Road, walking distance to Elaine's old school so she could finish second grade. They started looking for a piece of property to build a house on. The main criterion was that it had to be in the country. No more city living for them!

They found the perfect lot at 4512 W. Maple Road, a large corner lot of one and a half acres. Across the road were a farm and large fields reminding them of Iowa. Joe drew up house plans and found a builder from Flushing to construct their dream home.

Home designed by Joe in 1955

Joe was busy with the responsibilities of his new job and getting the new home finished in time for Elaine to start third grade at Mary Crapo Elementary in Swartz Creek. Elaine had missed her parents terribly when they left her in Iowa with her aunt and uncle,

156

and now the prospect of going to another school made her nervous. Her new teacher, Mrs. Faler, was very strict, and there were so many new faces. Elaine was being picked on and in phonics class she was getting a D, when she had been getting very good grades in all her classes at McKinley Elementary.

Evelyn was very involved in putting the finishing touches on their new home. She worked on the yard and planted tulips, daffodils, peonies, and irises. A great cook, she always prepared a meat-and-potatoes meal along with a scrumptious dessert for Joe when he got home from work. She volunteered at Elaine's school and the Red Cross, and was a Girl Scout leader. She took classes in the Bishop Method of sewing, and became certified as a master seamstress, making most of Elaine's school clothes. She modeled in a fashion show where she wore a large hat and a beautiful black dress she designed. To overcome her shyness, Evelyn took a Dale Carnegie public speaking course. Not only did she help sew the outfits for her group's final presentation, but also, she was stunned when she won the award for best speech.

Red Cross volunteer

Speaking at Dale Carnegie

Even though Joe took time to do jobs around the home and the irksome job of mowing the lawn, he much preferred fishing or experimenting in his spare time. His tinkering resulted in three original patents of his own. The patents granted to him by the government gave him the exclusive right to manufacture or sell his original inventions for 17 years. One was for *Thermostatically Controlled Cooling Systems for Internal Combustion Engines*; another was for a *Furnace Draft Control*; the third was for a *Thermostatically Controlled Mixing Valve*.

None of his patents made him any profit, but he did take great pride in having invented something that the U.S. Patent Law "recognized as a new useful process, machine, improvement, etc., that did not exist previously and that is recognized as the product of some unique intuition or genius, as distinguished from ordinary mechanical skill or craftsmanship."

Joe fishing   Joe tinkering

Then in January 1954, an entire island was vaporized by a hydrogen bomb the United States exploded in the Pacific. The Soviet Union was not far behind in testing a similar H-bomb in September of 1954. These hydrogen bombs were 1,000 times more powerful than the atomic bomb dropped on Hiroshima, and produced a frightening amount of deadly radioactive fallout.

At school, Elaine and her classmates were drilled to "duck and cover" in the event of a nuclear attack. At the GM factory where Joe worked, bomb shelters were designated for workers. The threat of a nuclear war generated by the Cold War between the United States and the Soviet Union created an uneasiness causing Joe to heed the Eisenhower administration's warnings regarding the devastation an atomic bomb could wreak. Like many Americans, Joe built a concrete block underground fallout shelter in the backyard of his new home to protect his family. It held water and supplies they would need for the recommended two-week stay in the event of a disaster. Fortunately, Joe's family and the country never had to put their shelters to the test.

Automation Engineer

Back on the job and in his new home, Joe was relieved General Motors had taken him back and he was again making good money. He was located in the Chevrolet Framing and Stamping Plant that supplied fenders, hoods, and frames to the assembly plant. The presses in Framing and Stamping were huge and terribly noisy. It was years before they installed silencers on the mammoth machines, much to the detriment of the hearing of those working there. But even though the working environment at this plant left a lot to be desired and working second shift wasn't conducive to family life, Joe felt working as an automation engineer was the best job he had had.

In this plant, numerous operations were performed on large sheets of metal at different stations. When an operation was completed, the metal was moved to the shipping department and loaded onto freight trains. As Joe recollected, "It was very greasy in the building and the workers had to wear thick leather gloves with pads to prevent their hands from getting sliced while working with the sharp metal."

Joe developed a process to separate the huge rolls of sheet metal, which were first cut into blanks, then coated in oil and fed into the massive thirty-foot-tall press machine to cut the needed shapes. Suction cups picked up and fed the heavy sheet metal pieces one at a time into the press. Then the metal went through a draw die press, "the biggest SOB in the plant," according to Joe. That machine stamped out the required parts. Even with the oil, the metal sheets would stick together. And that cost GM money.

Joe came up with a process where an air gun made a dimple in the corners of the blank sheets. The small dents allowed the sheets of metal to be easily separated and picked up one at a time, drawing them into the press. His idea resulted in a patent for a *Method and Apparatus for Separating Sheet Materials*, which saved a considerable amount of time and money for GM. The patent was company property. According to Joe, "General Motors millions instituting my ideas over the years."

Front fender blank separator   **Air tool forming dimple in blank**

Another idea Joe worked on was a method to reduce glare on rear-view mirrors. The backs of these mirrors flipped for night viewing and were covered with a silver coating. Joe found using black paint instead greatly reduced the glare. His simple idea was quickly adopted for all GM rear-view mirrors.

Joe was also given a difficult assignment for a company General Motors had taken over in 1954, the Euclid Company of Ohio. Their specialty was heavy earthmoving equipment. Ever ingenious in figuring out problems, Joe never thought his job ended the minute he left the plant at the end of his shift. He continued to think about how to solve the problems and often worked on them at home. Joe got a big rush when he finally figured out a solution to the Euclid problem, especially when others had been stymied by it.

Senior Automation Engineer

It wasn't long before Joe's hard work and ability to solve problems were recognized and he was promoted to senior automation engineer. In this position, there was no dearth of opportunities to try his ideas. And he had a lot of ideas! And like most inventors, some of his ideas were very successful and some of them weren't.

 (top-left rotated text)
made

J. DEW
SENIOR ENG.-AUTOMATION

GM patented his design for a shipping rack with an inflatable strap. The vehicle hood panels were loaded onto a rack and a strap secured the top and the open end. When the specially made belt was inflated, it kept the panels from shifting and being damaged during shipment in flatcars. Once the racks were off-loaded from the train, the hoods were easily removed when the air was released from the strap.

Hood rack with inflatable strap

One idea that didn't work was when Joe tried to improve the system to make automobile frames. Joe's idea was to change the sequence of the steps and hope it would improve productivity. As Joe recalled, "Unfortunately, that idea broke the machine all to the devil."

As senior automation engineer, Joe was often called in to troubleshoot even on his days off, which took precious time away from home and family. If a cam for a loader got out of adjustment, the loader would not function properly and as a consequence shut down the line. The result was lost production and lost money.

One Sunday, Joe was called in because of a loader breakdown. He rolled up his sleeves and figured out where the problem was and how to repair it. He drilled a hole through the cams and welded a rod through the hole to hold it in place. Sure enough, the problem was fixed. He was exasperated the next day when he was called into his boss's office and was chewed out for being so hands on. Joe shrugged his shoulders and accepted the criticism. Just part of the job he didn't agree with and found very frustrating!

Another challenge in the factory included conveyors that only went straight. Joe designed a conveyor to snake around corners and allow for easier and more efficient loading of fenders onto boxcars. His idea greatly increased productivity. Those kinds of positive results made the work rewarding and fun for Joe.

One more of Joe's innovative ideas was for an automatic spark timing control. His idea resulted in a GM patent for a mechanism to advance the timing as an engine sped up, which allowed for a smoother ride. For this patent, he was thrilled to receive his first bonus.

In spite of the many frustrations in dealing with problems and certain people in the work environment, Joe found the creative stimulus of being an automation engineer exceptionally fulfilling. He was proud of his contributions to making General Motors a leader in the automotive industry.

In addition to successes at work, Joe and Evelyn had good news on the home front. In 1957, Joe and Evelyn sat ten-year-old Elaine down in the living room to discuss a trade after she lost a tooth. "There's *no* tooth fairy!" she protested. Her little face scrunched up ready to cry, then she learned she was going to be a big sister. Something she had wanted for a very long time. She was so happy, as were Joe and Evelyn.

Dennis Joseph Dew arrived March 17, 1958. Joe and Evelyn were overjoyed at the birth of their son. Because of visiting rules, Elaine was unable to go into the hospital to see her mother and her new baby brother during her mother's weeklong stay. Joe took Elaine to the parking lot, where she looked up at the hospital window, blew kisses, and wildly waved at her mother. The family was finally complete.

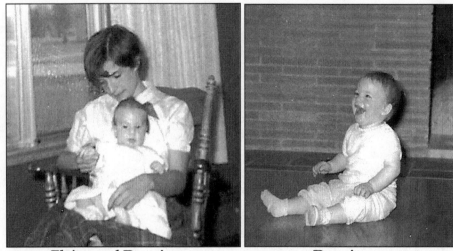

Elaine and Dennis   Dennis

Superintendent of Production

Joe took a week of vacation off while Evelyn was in the hospital. He got her and the baby settled at home, but needed to get back to work. In many ways, gaining promotions at General Motors was a game, and plant politics played a big part. Joe was willing to do his level best, work hard, and take work home. He was even willing to do things he felt were worthwhile like donating blood or mentoring a new employee, but he wouldn't get involved in the backstabbing, lying, and puffing up, a practice among others he found abhorrent. Joe was a straight shooter and didn't like the game playing.

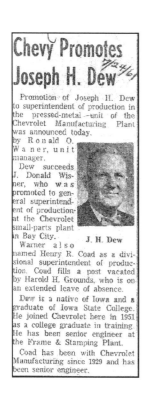
According to him, "I wouldn't kiss anybody's backside to advance myself." In fact, he prided himself on his honesty and in telling it like it was. In spite of this, he finally was promoted in 1961 to the next level, Superintendent of Production in the Pressed Metal unit of the Chevrolet Manufacturing Plant in Flint. This promotion put him on first shift, a change he truly appreciated. As one of the perks of this promotion, he got a new company car every three months. For this poor Iowa country boy, the financial security for his family meant a lot.

Family Life

Being on first shift allowed Joe more time at home with his family. Dennis, now three, with a ready smile and full of fun, was growing fast, and fourteen-year-old Elaine had just started high school. Although Joe's new job involved much more responsibility, it was a good increase in pay and allowed the family to have more opportunities to travel with three weeks of vacation each year.

Elaine, Dennis, Joe

Over the years, the family took yearly trips back to Iowa to visit relatives and Aunt Goldie. They enjoyed camping trips, pitching their tent in nearly every state in the nation. They held off bears at a cabin by beautiful Lake of the Clouds in the Porcupine Mountains State Park in Upper Michigan, crawled through Mammoth Cave in Kentucky, hiked through a moss forest along the picturesque Bay of Fundy in Nova Scotia, and camped near the ocean in Key West, Florida. Joe and Evelyn loved the outdoors and instilled a love of nature in their children.

Aunt Goldie, Dennis   **Florida vacation**

They explored the New York World's Fair and had a special treat of waffles with strawberries and whipped cream at the Belgium Village. Of course, they had to go on the popular General Motors seventeen-minute ride at the Futurama exhibit, which took them to the moon, the Antarctic, the bottom of the sea, through the desert, atop mountains, and to a dream city of the future. It was quite an exciting and unforgettable event.

For Elaine's graduation, they took an adventure-filled trip to Disneyland in California. The first night of the trip, it was pouring rain so hard the family stayed in a motel. The second night, they ended up in the mountains far from civilization as the sky turned a rosy orange and the sun dipped below the horizon. They got their tent out, only to find Joe had forgotten to pack the tent poles. It was a memorable night sleeping on the ground with the distant stars twinkling above them in the pitch-black night sky. The next day, Joe found some saplings and whittled the needed poles. In New Mexico, they saw cascading stalactites, huge pillar stalagmites, and hundreds of bats clinging to the cave ceiling in Carlsbad Caverns.

After camping overnight in the desert, their next stop, the Pacific Ocean, looked very inviting. Unfortunately, the camp sites were all taken and they had to travel into the foothills. They pitched their tent after dark and tiredly crawled into bed only to be awakened by

Elaine's screams. Perched on her blanket was a big scorpion with its tail arched over its head in attack position. They must have picked it up the night before when camping in the Mojave Desert. Poor Elaine's arm swelled to nearly twice its size, but with a few aspirin, she would be fine. Going to the doctor for a little problem wasn't considered a necessity.

A walk along the Pacific Ocean, magical Disneyland, and a night in a hotel with a pool and slide, Knott's Berry Farm with adorable goats and the bumpy Calico Mine ride through barely lit tunnels of a working gold mine! They were all wonderful places to visit! The final stop before heading home was to see the truly magnificent towering redwoods.

Like all families, they had their challenging times. At the age of four, Dennis developed Perthes of the hip. It was a rare childhood condition where there was a loss of blood supply to the head of his femur and necessitated he spend a long stretch in a wheelchair. Then he had to use braces for months. Evelyn battled a rare form of breast cancer at the young age of 40, with Joe steadfastly at her side. Shortly thereafter, she developed rheumatoid arthritis, which plagued her for the rest of her life. Joe's older sister, Arlene, died suddenly from a cerebral aneurysm at the age of 48, just months after the family's fun-filled trip to California.

They also had their share of joys. Elaine married her high school sweetheart Larry Briggs and headed off to college at Michigan State University, although seven-year-old Dennis missed his big sister terribly. Joe remembered the thrill of driving a fast red Corvette at the Milford Proving Grounds. An especially happy occasion was when Joe bought the old homestead in Iowa where he and his family had lived along the railroad tracks. The home remained, but was unlivable. On their frequent visits to Iowa to see family, they enjoyed walking around the 17 acres. Joe was happy he could share his childhood haunts with his son. He even took Dennis hunting for morels in the spring as he had done as a lad.

Homestead 1985

Life was going well. Joe was overjoyed, grinning ear to ear when he came home to tell Evelyn he received a promotion to General Superintendent of Production at Flint Pressed Metal Division. This position put him in charge of four plants with a lot more responsibilities and included a sizeable raise. Joe was feeling very confident about their future.

A New Home

Fourteen years after building their home on Maple Road, the area became much less peaceful, with more houses being built and much more traffic. The increased car exhaust aggravated Evelyn's allergies resulting in frequent headaches. A subdivision was built on the farmland across the road from them. Numerous accidents at their intersection woke them in the middle of the night and sent them scurrying to help. Once again, Joe and Evelyn decided they needed more fresh, open, country air.

They found property twelve miles away, at 11015 W. Baldwin Road in Gaines, land in the same school district for Dennis. It had a beautiful hill to build the house on and 27 acres for farming. Dennis was over-the-moon excited too. It meant he would finally be able to get a dog.

Just as they decided on the design for the new home, Joe got a call from his brother John with news of the passing of their dear Aunt Belle at age 75. Joe and family headed back to Iowa to attend the funeral and her burial near her parents in Jefferson Cemetery, Jefferson, Iowa.

Belle Dew

With the coming of spring, Joe and Evelyn were ready to begin work on their new home. Ever frugal, despite Joe's executive position, they did a lot of the work themselves. And even though Dennis was only eleven, he helped with building their new home. When they went to pick up his black lab, Dennis was ecstatic to have his new puppy!

Joe with new puppy at site of new home
170

Work on their new house began with Joe designing the trusses as he had for the mess hall at Schnee Eifel during the war. "Climbing the ladder and hoisting the heavy trusses into place sure was scary," recalled Dennis. "Dad and I worked side by side. I pounded in what seemed like thousands of nails." Joe did all the electrical work except for putting in the fuse box. He also saved by putting in all the plumbing himself. Evelyn was kept busy, too. One day, tired and with frustrations running particularly high, she lobbed a hammer at Joe after he made and especially sarcastic remark. She was later thankful she hadn't hit him.

For the time, Joe was extraordinarily progressive in recycling and being green. To insulate the entire house, he hauled home Styrofoam die molds, salvaged from the trash pile at the factory. He installed a grid of pipes in the back of the fireplace to heat the water running through the grid and circulated it throughout the home's heat runs: a big saving on energy in the winter months! He embedded flexible black plastic tubing in the concrete patio that he painted dark green. Water was pumped through the tubing, thus using solar power to heat the water for the pool.

Joe, Evelyn, and Dennis invested a lot of sweat equity in building their new home. When their two-bedroom house was done, Joe and his family happily moved. The acreage allowed Joe to get a small Ford tractor and putter at farming. He tinkered on his ideas in the workshop, a relief from the stresses at his job. Especially nice was the solitude of the country to raise their son.

Pool with wasp's nest on wall

Solar patio before painted dark green

Windmills

Another green interest and passion of Joe's since he was young was wind power. Their little farm permitted him the space to enthusiastically pursue his interest in inventing a more perfect windmill. Even on trips back to Iowa, he took time to research at the Iowa State University in Ames. There he found a useful and relatively rare pamphlet he studiously read, *Horizontal Windmills, Draft Mills and Similar Air-flow Engines*, written by Greville Bathe in 1948.

With all the information he garnered from many sources, Joe designed a zero-pitch wind turbine using parts scavenged from the junk yard. The windmill had an egg beater design with three propellers and a governor to control the speed of the blades. He used a die grinder to carefully carve the blades and added a tail to swing it out of the wind. He meticulously did all the gearing himself, mounting a gear box at the top of the telephone pole in his yard and connected it to a drive shaft running down the side of the pole. The drive shaft was connected to a transmission (a used rear car axle) with a 10:1 ratio. Every spin of the windmill equaled ten spins of the generator. Then from the generator, Joe ran a cable into the basement utility room.

He hadn't been sure his wind turbine would work, but was pleased when it ran like a charm. It generated enough for a heating coil to make his morning coffee. People often stopped at the house to ask about the curious windmill, which, Dennis named *Dooz Demon*. And one stormy night, it lived up to its name.

Some of Joe's windmill experiments

The sky darkened and the wind began blowing so fiercely Joe couldn't pull the chain hard enough to wrest the windmill out of the wind. Dennis was down at his buddy's house when the phone rang. His dad yelled into the phone he needed help with the turbine, "Come home NOW!"

Dennis jumped in his car and quickly drove the mile home through pounding rain. But even with the two of them, they couldn't pull hard enough to get the propeller swung out of the wind. Kaboom! The propeller exploded off! The next day, they found pieces of it 300 yards away with a long, sharp piece of the propeller embedded in the neighbor's tree. They were exceptionally fortunate no one had been hurt!

A Shocking Turn of Events

Joe had settled in and was enjoying his executive position as General Superintendent of Production, making sure things in the four plants were running smoothly. They had a lovely new home and life was feeling "pretty darn good." That was why it came as such a blow when he was told he was being promoted to Director of Safety in 1970. According to the Occupational Safety and Health Administration, Joe's job as the administrator of industrial hygiene was "to anticipate, recognize, evaluate, and recommend controls for environmental and physical hazards that can affect the health and well-being of workers." The supposed "promotion" felt more like a demotion to him. He was more than qualified for the job, but he went from a Grade 10 to a Grade 8. It was definitely a step down to a dead-end job and a huge disappointment to Joe.

Joe at safety meeting

This new position was necessitated by the government's enactment of the Occupational Safety and Health Act, which President Nixon signed into law on December 29, 1970. As Director of Safety, Joe had to make sure the OSHA requirements for all North American General Motors plants were met. He traveled to Canada and plants all over the United States making sure General Motors "assured safe and healthful working conditions for working men and women by setting and enforcing standards and by providing training, outreach, education and assistance." Joe had never particularly liked traveling and being away from family which was required by this job. He did the new job and did it well, but it was a job he decidedly did not enjoy as much as his previous position.

Brother John, Merrill's Marauders

Shortly after Joe's job change, he began to worry about his brother John. Joe was close to his older brother and kept in touch with him, always visiting him on trips back to Iowa. He knew John had had a difficult time in World War II fighting with the 475th Infantry Regiment, better known as Merrill's Marauders.

Shortly after the attack on Pearl Harbor, John had made the trip from Redfield, Iowa to Des Moines to join the army. He volunteered to be an infantryman assigned to light mortars with the 475th Infantry Regiment, Mars Task Force, fighting the Japanese in India, Burma, and China during World War II.

It was an all-volunteer unit that began its combat journey in Calcutta, India. John's unit fought against the Japanese in the heat of soggy jungles and across cold, rugged, mountainous terrain. In an effort to lighten loads for the mules carrying supplies and munitions through the treacherous territory, the men constantly ate unappetizing K rations. John told Joe, "After weeks and weeks, those K rations sure didn't taste very good."

On their long-range missions, often behind enemy lines, dangers lurked not only from the enemy, but from serious illnesses as well. John contracted malaria as he fought during a march over hundreds of miles in one of the worst monsoon seasons ever recorded, with over 375 inches of rain that inundated the troops over a twelve-week period. Joe remembered John telling him, "There were times you couldn't see your hands right in front of your face, because it was raining so hard."

Out of the 2,750 men who began the campaign in Burma with John, only two survived who had not been hospitalized with wounds or a major illness like amoebic dysentery, typhus, malaria, and any number of fevers. Although the Japanese forces often outnumbered them, John's unit inflicted a great number of casualties on the enemy. John and his buddies fought hard while suffering more hunger, fevers, and disease on their long-range missions than any other U.S. Army unit during World War II.

Private First Class John Dew received the Combat Infantry Badge, the World War II Victory Medal, the Army Good Conduct Medal, the American Campaign Medal, the Asiatic Pacific Campaign Medal, and the Bronze Star for acts of heroism, acts of merit, and meritorious service in a combat zone, as did each and every member of the unit. Joe knew John's sacrifice, along with countless others in the Allied forces, helped defeat the aggression of the Axis powers. Had it not been for them, so many lives would be much different today.

John in India

Early in 1972, John told Joe he had sought help at the Veterans Health Administration Medical Center in Des Moines, only to be told there was nothing they could do to help him escape the never-ending pain in his head. Joe was angry with the VA for not helping John and was outraged at the lack of care given to him.

Then on November 27, 1972, John could not deal with the severe headaches any longer and made the tragic decision to end his own life. He was only 60 years old. Stunned by the loss of his brother, Joe was very angry with the Veteran's Administration doctors and felt they had contributed to John's death through negligence. John would always be a hero in Joe's eyes and he would miss him. His was a grievous loss.

A Difficult Decision

Joe was adrift after his brother's death. In his grief, Joe lacked enthusiasm for his work at General Motors. He did not find his position as Director of Safety satisfying at all. On December 1, 1974, Roger B. Smith was appointed executive vice-president in charge of the financial, public relations, and various government relations staff. Smith felt General Motors needed to replace older workers with younger ones.

Subsequently, the same year, Joe was offered a buyout. When he arrived home from work, Evelyn could tell by the look on his face something was wrong. Joe plunked down on the couch and tersely explained what had happened. He was upset and so was she. It was devastating news to their plans for their future. Dennis wasn't even out of high school yet. Joe vividly remembered how Evelyn hugged him tight and cried her eyes out.

Ever the realist, Joe sat down and figured out the economics of retiring. Waiting a few more years seemed financially prudent, but he realized his future was uncertain with General Motors. If he stayed, there were no guarantees about what position they would give him or if he could retire later with the perks the current buyout offered.

In the end, he and Evelyn woefully decided it was in their best interest to accept the deal. At the young age of 55, after 25 years with General Motors, he was out. The shop had been a rough place to work. As Joe recounted, "It wasn't a particularly nice place for either hourly or salary workers." He knew he had been conscientious in all the positions he had held while at General Motors and had made a positive contribution. There was a party for him and well wishes from his colleagues. Joe was sorry to leave on such a sour note, but according to him, "I never regretted the decision one bit."

CHEVROLET MOTOR DIVISION

General Motors Corporation ☐ 30007 Van Dyke Avenue ☐ Warren, Michigan 48090

Office of the General Manufacturing Manager   January 15, 1975

Dear Joe:

It was with some surprise I heard from George Johnson you would be retiring in February.

I want to thank you personally for the work you have done these past two years in coordinating the activities of the Michigan plants related to OSHA and environmental activities.

The time you spent with our plant people and Government bodies has been a great help to Chevrolet in meeting their commitments to improve our plants and facilities.

Your interpretation of the OSHA regulations and the work that you did to have the regulations changed or modified to provide more meaningful coverage, has been a real asset.

I hope you will enjoy many years of a healthy, happy retirement.

                    Sincerely,

                    Jim

                    J. W. McLERNON

Mr. J. H. Dew
Chevrolet Motor Division
Flint-Pressed Metal Plant
Flint, Michigan

Good wishes retirement letter

Life after General Motors

Evelyn and Joe

Retirement

The first Monday morning Joe woke up after retiring, he was pleased he didn't have to jump out of bed and put on a suit and tie. The house was quiet. Dennis had already left for school. Evelyn fixed them coffee and they sat peacefully looking out over the fields. He had lots of odd jobs to catch up on as well as pursuing his dream of inventing a better windmill. The stresses of frequently flying off to a new city, staying in hotels, and leaving his family to troubleshoot problem after problem for General Motors were over.

Then a short month after he retired, Joe was jolted by a call from his younger brother's wife. Only a few days before his 45th birthday, Jim dropped dead from a heart attack. A rare late-April snowstorm---the second biggest snowstorm on record in Flint, with 17.3 inches of snow---prevented Joe and Evelyn from going to his funeral in Port Huron. Of Joe's six brothers and sisters, only his older sister Goldie and his sister Echo remained alive. It was definitely a shock and it validated his decision to retire and spend more time with family, and enjoy life.

In June, Joe and Dennis packed to go to the Second U.S. National Conference on Wind Engineering Research at Fort Collins, Colorado. At age 17, Dennis was able to help with the driving on the long trip. He even got a taste of college life while staying with his dad in the dorm at Colorado State University.

In their free time, they took in the sights and the beauty of the mountainous area. They drove by a ranch Joe had worked on when he was a teenager bumming around the country. At a park, they hiked a trail to a lookout over the gorge. As Joe stood gazing into the distance and holding on to a metal railing, there was a surprisingly loud crack and he was knocked on his rear. A bolt of lightning had struck Joe while Dennis, who stood only a few feet away, was unhurt. Joe was momentarily stunned and had a burn mark the size of a large thumb print on his head. "I had one heck of a headache and my body ached all over, but I was okay," he recalled.

It was the third time in his life he had been struck by lightning. Once he had been hit near the big tree in the pasture at the homestead and once while practicing on the Redfield High School football field. Fortunately, each time he wasn't hurt badly. But he knew the power of lightning and he knew how lucky he had been. He hoped the third time would be the last.

Joe found the workshops at the conference most enlightening and was excited by the cutting-edge information in this new field of study. He was eager to head home and use some of the new information he had learned to pursue his goal of creating a patent for a more effective wind turbine that hopefully would be profitable. After the conference, he refined his ideas through correspondence with an aeronautical engineer who he had met there. He even built a wind tunnel to test his ideas.

Joe continued his experiments over the years to develop a better wind turbine and filed a Disclosure Document with the Patent Office in 1980. Through this program, the Patent Office kept the document detailing Joe's "Wind Generator Speed Control" for two years. The Disclosure Document provided legal protection and evidence of the conception of his invention and awaited his filing of a patent. (However, no documents were found that indicated he had eventually filed a patent on his wind generator speed control.)

Joe applied for a position with the Department of Energy when President Jimmy Carter created his 12th cabinet-level department. Energy and conservation were big areas of interest for Joe. Through the DOE, proposals were solicited with hopes of developing new energy technology, in part as a response to the energy crisis of the 1970s. Joe's application was accepted and he was hired as a consultant to read and evaluate energy proposals. He found the work very interesting and was able to complete it from home.

Family

In 1976, Dennis graduated from high school and married his high school sweetheart, Janice Todd. He got a job as a welder at Metal

Fabrication in Flint, and after a few months, realized welding was not what he wanted to do with the rest of his life. He enrolled at Mott Community College and secured a job at F&E Manufacturing as a draftsman. After finishing his associate's degree in engineering, Dennis got an internship as a die maker's apprentice at Fisher Body Metal Fabricating and moved to Grand Rapids. Another Dew working for General Motors! A very proud moment for Joe and Evelyn!

Dennis

Joe and Evelyn continued to enjoy traveling after Dennis married. Being retired and with an empty nest, they were able to take even longer trips. They decided to make a luxury purchase, one they saved for and paid for with cash. They never had a credit card and always saved until they had enough, even for the big items.

With their savings, they bought a small Boler trailer they pulled with their new Chevy Citation, General Motor's first front-wheel-drive compact car. Although the trailer was only thirteen feet long, it had all the amenities they needed for an enjoyable camping experience. The bed certainly was more comfortable than sleeping in a tent on an air mattress on the hard ground. Evelyn liked the

182

small propane gas range and small refrigerator, even though they ate the majority of their meals out while camping.

Grandchildren added to their retirement joys. Elaine had two sons, Jeff and Brian, and Dennis had two sons, Joshua and Nathan. Evelyn loved Christmas and always made it a magical holiday with special handmade ornaments and gifts for the family. She was a great cook and made holiday feasts and she always included the grandkids' favorites: delicious homemade macaroni and cheese, homemade cheesecake, double cruncher cookies, and cherry pie for dessert. When Jeff and Brian graduated from high school, Evelyn made hundreds of cookies for the graduation party guests. Both Joe and Evelyn loved being grandparents.

Dennis, Nate, Josh

Joe, Dennis, Janice, Nate, Josh 1991

Joe, Jeff, Evelyn at MSU graduation

Brian with HS grad cookies Evelyn made

Medical Concerns

During the holidays when Joe turned 62, he hadn't been himself. He was tired all the time, taking a lot of naps, and just didn't seem to have any energy. Evelyn was very worried about him. Finally, in January when he was sitting at the kitchen table and grimacing from pain, she put her foot down. "I don't want any arguments," she said firmly, "I'm taking you to the emergency room!" Joe didn't argue.

Doctors found Joe was bleeding internally and rushed him to emergency surgery. He was in a tremendous amount of pain and feeling very weak. According to him, "I even considered that perhaps my time was up. After all, ever since the war, I felt that I was living on borrowed time."

The surgeon removed a large cancerous tumor the size of a grapefruit and stopped the bleeding. Fortunately, the cancer hadn't spread and was contained within the intestine. By the next evening, Joe was sitting up and happily eating meatloaf and mashed potatoes. Chemotherapy treatments followed, which made him quite sick, but fortunately, there was no recurrence of the cancer.

Evelyn had her share of medical troubles too. Although rheumatoid and osteoarthritis ravaged her body with constant pain, it never stopped her from taking care of the home, traveling, sewing, doing the hobbies she loved, and making time for her family. The disease made her hands and feet painfully swollen and twisted. None of the treatments Evelyn had tried for her rheumatoid arthritis worked particularly well. With a great deal of hope, she tried gold injections. However, the doctor didn't monitor her as closely as he should have and she ended up in the hospital for more than a week, nearly dying from her reaction to the gold shots.

She eventually had to have the knuckles in her left foot and right hand replaced with artificial joints. They traveled to have the surgery done by a specialist in Grand Rapids, who was considered the top in the country. After her release from Blodgett Hospital, they stopped to visit Dennis and family in Whalen, just south of Grand Rapids, before heading home to Flint.

The temperatures were frigid and when they turned on the country road, they found it was pure ice. After finishing their visit, they drove out of the driveway and down the hill. Joe put on the brakes for the stop sign at the foot of the hill, but the car skidded and went flying, flipped over, and landed in the little creek. Wearing seat belts is what saved their lives.

Joe was able to climb out of the car and trudge up to Dennis' home on the top of the hill, where they got the sled and hauled Evelyn safely back to the house. Fortunately, they were both only bruised and shaken. Definitely not what you want to have happen after surgery, but they both were in one piece and considered themselves lucky to have no broken bones and only minor car repairs.

Then ten years after Joe retired, he was diagnosed with Type II diabetes. The doctor advised him if he wanted to avoid major health problems from the diabetes, he needed to change his diet and lose weight. And that's just what he did! It took him a while and his plan was rather unconventional, but he accomplished his goal. And that kept the diabetes at bay.

Joe had three main ideas about how best to lose weight and keep it off. He even wrote an article he submitted to *Reader's Digest* for publication. To quote him, "First, find the time of day you can best go without food and use it to your advantage. Second, when you do eat, give your stomach big volumes of low-calorie/low-carbohydrate foods. A full stomach isn't hungry. And third, if tempted in between meals, stave off hunger with low-calorie beverages."

He followed his advice, even buying ten cases at a time of Diet Rite pop from a local warehouse. He drank it to stave off the hunger and used it on his cereal in place of milk. It took time, but he managed to go from 240 pounds to 180 pounds: a loss of 60 pounds! He felt good that his diabetes was under control. No pills, no insulin injections. It was a weight loss he proudly maintained for the rest of his life.

In spite of his weight loss, Joe continued to have high blood pressure and trouble with high triglycerides. Several years later, he ended up in the hospital with what the doctor said was a coronary artery spasm heart attack. He began to limit sodium intake, but found it exceptionally difficult. Growing up during the Great Depression, salt had been used liberally at every meal to season an often bland diet and was a habit he had continued into adulthood.

His daughter Elaine tried to convince him to eat better and change his lifestyle to manage some of the medical problems he was having, but he wasn't easily convinced. When Joe and Evelyn came to Elaine's house to watch their dog while she and her husband Larry went on vacation, she left several books for him, hoping he would pick them up and read them. And he did! He was most impressed with *A Thorn in the Starfish: The Immune System and How It Works* by Robert S. Desowitz.

Elaine was pleased it actually convinced him of the scientific value of healthy eating. He changed his eating habits and started taking vitamins, becoming an avid reader and believer in the power of vitamins. He became open to alternative treatments and successfully tried chelation therapy for a 75 percent blocked carotid artery. After treatment, he was checked and his carotid arteries showed "no significant stenosis." An amazing improvement!

In February 1986, the Des Moines hospital contacted Joe with the sad news his sister Goldie had been admitted and was in serious condition. He and Evelyn rushed to Iowa. It wasn't good. Goldie had advanced colon cancer and died three days after their arrival. On February 27, 1986, Joe's beloved sister, Goldie, was laid to rest next to their sister DeElda and parents in the East Linn Cemetery in Redfield, Iowa.

Goldie Dew

Taken by Jeff and Brandie Briggs

After the funeral, the family recalled some of their treasured memories of Aunt Goldie. Trips from Iowa on the train to visit, walks and talks, lots of letter writing back and forth, Christmas gifts of Yonker's candy from where she had worked. She had been very close to Elaine and Dennis and was greatly missed. One cute story they told was when Joe gave Goldie her first television in 1958. She got a real kick out of it. Then in 1969, he got her a new color television against her protests. "I don't need a color TV!" she vehemently protested. But she called all aflutter and excited after the TV arrived and she had watched her first television show in vibrant color. When Goldie retired from Yonkers in Des Moines, Joe sent her a generous check and wrote, "Now use the check to be extravagant with your utilities, etc... Love, Your brother Joe." Goldie Dew was a kind, sweet, caring lady. Joe had always loved and looked out for his big sister and would dearly miss her, as would the rest of the family.

Another Move

Goldie's death hit Joe hard. Although he had had colon cancer and a heart attack, the reality, the actual eventuality of his own death, hadn't truly hit home. This was different, and he felt his mortality. As with other decisions in his life, Joe discussed things with Evelyn. He worried if he were to die, she would be left alone out in the country with too much to manage. Within a few months of Goldie's death, Joe and Evelyn decided to sell their home and acreage in the country and move to an apartment closer to Flint.

On Thursday, May 29, 1986, Joe and Evelyn watched as household belongings, tools, and farm equipment were auctioned off. They were leaving the home they had built, and although they knew this was what needed to be done, they would miss their home in the country.

FARM MACHINERY, TOOLS
HOUSEHOLD
AUCTION
11015 W. BALDWIN RD.
Located in Gaines, Michigan. Take Grand Blanc Road west to Nichols Road, south on Nichols Road to Baldwin Road.
MR. & MRS. JOSEPH H. DEW, Owners
THURSDAY, MAY 29, 4:00 p.m.
FARM EQUIPMENT: Ford 2000 tractor, 1440 hours; Ford 2-bottom plow; Ford 10' disc; rotary hoe; cultivator; cultipacker; bush-hog mower; sprayer; grain drill; small 2-wheel trailer; Ford scoop; Ford blade; clod buster; Cub Cadet 38" mower; post drill; TOOLS: Power Kraft drill press; bench vise; hand tools; 10" DeWalt table saw; 1/2" Craftsman drill; Craftsman skil saw; Wen sander; Wen planer; HOUSEHOLD AND MISCELLANEOUS: Platform rocker; maple dining room table; kitchen table w/4 chairs; colonial maple rocker; hassock; roll-away bed; Zenith B&W TV; maple dining room chairs (5); Singer sewing machine, cabinet; card table; Single bedframe w/mattress; large metal desk w/swivel chair; maple drop-leaf end table; folding chairs; aluminum folding cots; boy's bike; rocking horse; Hoover vacuum; encyclopedias; luggage; old clock; horse collars; 3 old cast-iron stoves; dishes; toaster oven, pots and pans; Elgin boat motor; upholstered chairs; wheelbarrow; ladders; ice cream freezer; pictures
AUCTIONEERS NOTE: This merchandise and farm equipment has been well taken care of. Lunch on premises.
BOB CANADAY AUCTIONEER
Sales & Service (313) 635-7260

LOVELY RANCH (Rear View) With indoor pool. Must see this unusual ranch on 26.6 acres. 2 bedrooms, 2 baths, walk-out basement with 2 car garage, 53'x28' Natorium. Baldwin Road, Swartz

In August, they moved to a one-bedroom apartment at Maple Park Terraces nearer Flint. It was a nice complex with lots of trees and a carport for their vehicle to help during Michigan's snowy winter months. There was a clubhouse and fitness center where Joe worked out each morning before they went to lunch. Their lives settled into a routine of meeting friends at Country Buffet for lunch six days a week and going to the library often.

Family activities were always a priority for them, and they continued to visit Dennis and his family in Grand Rapids and Elaine and Larry in Milan, as well as having the family Christmas get-togethers. They visited Evelyn's family in Iowa and took four-week long camping trips in the winter to get away from the cold, gray Michigan winters. They attended many class reunions and even traveled to several army reunions. In spite of a variety of health issues, they continued to live a full life, loving and taking care of each other.

Joe and Evelyn

Epilogue

Four years after moving to the apartment, Mom began having stomach problems. Eight months later, after numerous tests, continued problems, and finally surgery, she passed away from colon cancer the doctor had misdiagnosed. Dad forever missed his partner in life.

Dad's favorite picture of Evelyn kept by his chair

Dad kept busy with finding and repairing lamps, vacuum cleaners, and whatever else came his way to tinker with and fix up. He pursued his interests in reading about alternative health and science topics. He made many visits to see our family in Milan and Dennis and his family in Grand Rapids. He continued the routine of eating lunch at the Country Buffet with the lunch bunch.

A year after mom's passing, he met Lois at the Country Buffet and they became close friends. They enjoyed sharing lunches together and playing Rummikub, which sparked Dad's analytical mind and competitive spirit.

In 2000, he had a minor stroke and moved to independent living near our home in Milan, Michigan, where he charmed the staff with his polite and gentle ways. He enjoyed holidays with family. He lit up when he saw his great-grandchildren and had a special bond with his namesake, Michael Joseph Briggs. He called Dennis and talked to him every day. I visited frequently and continued to gather his stories. When I asked my father, "What is the most memorable part of your life?" I expected him to tell me about the war or the amazing things he had done in his years at General Motors. His answer touched me deeply. "The best part of my life was my family," he replied simply.

Elaine, Joe, and Dennis' sons Nate and Josh

Joe and great-grandson Tadd

Joe and Michael Joseph Briggs 1999

Kyle, Michael, Joe, Emily, Keith-great grandchildren

Following are the last two journal entries I wrote about my dad after his second stroke when he had to move from assisted living to the Saline Evangelical Home.

Journal Entry June 2013

Today I didn't leave the nursing home crying or merely exhausted. I left with a sense of awe at how my father continues to carry on with dignity at 83 with a bent body and a fading mind.

There perhaps is no more sinking feeling than to see your father, alone, at the end of a hall, slumped in his wheelchair, head uncomfortably bent. We start with the routine of hugs and "I love you, Dad." Move the clock from the far side of his room to a spot on the wall beside his bed; call his lady friend two time zones away now living with her children.

Jennifer Bond, one of the wonderful staff, greets us with a smile as we head down the hall. She cheerfully asks Dad, "Do you want to dance?" "I would if I could," Dad replies with a small smile as she bends down and gives him a hug. We roll on down the hall with a pillow pushing his tilting, left side a little more toward center. I am crunching the Rummikub game under my arm to manipulate the wheelchair through nurses' carts of meds, plastic bins, and a multitude of wheelchairs with the gentle souls of creased faces and age-wracked bodies.

The blare of call bells dim a bit, as we enter the cheery recreation room with its many plants and windows. Elegantly plumed Cairo greets us with a song. Bert and Ernie nibble lettuce in their cages. I dump out the Rummikub tiles and Dad laboriously begins reaching, grasping, and turning over each tile one by one until finally ready for the game.

I readjust the pillow at his side, but his tiring body won't stay upright. Then it hits me. A deep love, a sense of awe at how he keeps going, keeps trying, keeps living and finding some modicum

194

of contentment. Such a trooper. Never complaining. Never whining about what he's losing.

How can I do less? How can I not be a trooper, too? It's time to go.

"Good-bye, Dad. I love you."

"I love you, too."

"How much?"

"Oodles."

Journal Entry July 2003

When I arrived to visit Dad, he was lying in bed, covered with blankets, and with a white towel Jennifer had gently wrapped around his head to keep him warm.

He didn't want to get up, just said he was sleepy. I pulled up the chair beside him and sat by his side. After a while, he started talking. He was more lucid than he'd been in a number of days.

"This is a good way to go," he said. "I'm not in pain."

"You're not? You're just tired?" I asked with tears brimming in my eyes.

"No, sleepy," he replied. "Tell Dennis good-bye and that I love him."

"You're a good dad. I love you."

"I hope I haven't been too much bother to you."

"You haven't, Dad. I love you."

"I hope GM pays the insurance."

I smiled and shook my head. "Don't worry, Dad. I'll make sure they do."

"I love you, daughter. I'm ready for my next great adventure."

I sat with Dad as he faded into a deep sleep. Larry and my son Brian's wife Hedieh came. Dennis arrived from Grand Rapids. We sat with Dad until he was off on his "next great adventure."

My dad's story is complete and the promise I made fulfilled. His stories and the time we spent together were an extraordinary gift. His was, indeed, a glorious life.

Joe Dew 1945

The United States of America
honors the memory of

Joseph H Dew

This certificate is awarded by a grateful nation in recognition of devoted and selfless consecration to the service of our country in the Armed Forces of the United States.

President of the United States

George W. Bush Letter 2003

198

Appendices

A. Dew Family Tree

Richard Dewe & Elizabeth Keyt
? - >1539   ? -1542

Edward Dewe & Margaret
~1500-1558   ? -1570

From his hard work, Edward's family was the richest in Didcot with assets on his death in both livestock and arable farming, £70. At wife's death, assets were £102.

Richard Dewe & Margaret Sawyer
1530-1573   ? -1568

Richard, a yeoman, was the black sheep of the family, drank too much, and died bankrupt with 43 creditors.

Edward Dewe & Agnys Loder
1562-1632   Didcot, England

Edward was a hard-working yeoman. He invested in the Virginia Company and left shares to his grandsons and over £800.

Thomas Dewe & Annie Helms
1584-1624   1581-1635

Thomas was a guild stationer and sold books on Fleet Street in London, England.

Colonel Thomas Dewe & Elizabeth Bennett
1600-1691   1603-1667

After his father's death, Thomas took over the business. He used his grandfather's legacy to settle in the Virginia Colony. A British soldier, he battled Indians in the new settlement and was a successful tobacco plantation owner with extensive holdings in Virginia, NC and the Caribbean. As a Founding Father of Virginia, he was Speaker of the House of Burgesses and the Governor's Counselor. At age 72, he became a Quaker.

John Dew, Sr. & Elizabeth Shearer
1636-1678   ~1650- ~1700

He was educated in England and was a plantation owner in Virginia.

John Dew, Jr. Esq. & Susannah Shearer
1675-1744   ~1670- ~1744

He moved to North Carolina and owned large plantations along the Meherrin River.

Joseph Dew, Sr. & Constance Dew
1706 - <1760   ~1706- ~1758

Joseph Dew, Jr. & Violet Eastwood
1741-1808   1751-1831

In 1799, the Quaker family of 11 pioneered in Ohio Country.

Elias Dew & Sarah McMillan
1787- ~1870   1792-1840

He was a Quaker pioneer in Short Creek, Ohio.

Joseph H. Dew & Winifred Kirby
1818-1885   1819-1889

Joseph was a Quaker minister in Ohio.

John T. Dew & Mary Jane (Molly) Auld
1841-1902   1841-1927

He was a disabled Civil War veteran, 65th Indiana Volunteer Infantry. He married and moved to Iowa. He was a laborer due limits of his severe leg injury from the war.

Joseph L. Dew & Edna May Berg
1879-1946   1887-1947

Joseph was a blacksmith in Iowa. Edna's ancestors go back to Emperor Charlemagne.

Joseph H. Dew & Evelyn Johnston
1920-2003   1922-1990

Children:
 Dennis Joseph Dew   &   Ilene Elaine Dew (Briggs)
 (Janice Todd)   (Larry K. Briggs)

Grandchildren and Great-Grandchildren:
 -Joshua Aaron Dew   **-Jeffrey Joseph Briggs**
  -Liberty, Tregan, Trinity, Jonah   -Thaddeus, Keith, Kyle
 -Nathan Joseph Dew   **-Brian Keith Briggs**
                                                        -Emily, Michael

B. Joe Dew's Iowa State College Transcript

Transcript of the record of

Dew, Joseph Harold   Admitted Fall, 1937   Curriculum Engr.

From Redfield Consld. High School, Iowa   Present Address Ames, Iowa

ENTRANCE UNITS

						Entrance Conditions
Engl.	3½	Algebra	1½	G.Sci.	1	
Lang.		Plane Geometry	1	Miscel.	5	
History	1	Solid Geometry				
Civics	½	Trigonometry				
Economics	½	Agr.	1			
Sociology		Phys.	1			

COLLEGIATE RECORD

COURSE	QUARTER CREDITS	GRADE	COURSE	QUARTER CREDITS	GRADE
Fall, 1937			Phys. 221, General Phys.	5	A
Chem. 101a, General Chem.	4	Wxx	**Spring, 1948**		
Engl. 101, Freshman Comp.	3	D	E.E. 202, Dir. Curr. Machines	6	C
Math. 101, College Algebra	5	Dxx	Math. 212, Calculus	4	C
E.Dr. 131, Drawing & Projection	2	C	Phys. 222, General Phys.	5	B
Gen.E. 104, Engr. Problems	1	C	**Summer, 1948**		
P.E. 101, Phys.Educ.	R	C	Engl. 205, Prop.Anal.Reas.&Writ.	3	B
Engr. 114, Orientation	R	A	Sp. 311, Speech Making	3	C
Spring, 1938 – Changed to E.E.			Psych. 335, Educational Psych.	3	C
Chem. 101a, General Chem.	4	Dxx	**Fall, 1948 – Changed to Sci.**		
Engl. 102, Freshman Comp.	3	C	M.L. 261, Elem. Spanish	3	B
Math. 102c, Plane Trig.	4	Dxx	Zool. 104, General Biology	3	C
E.Dr. 132, Theory of Proj. Draw.	3	D	Ec. 384d, Accounting I	4	C
Gen.E. 105, Engr. Problems	1	Cxx	Engl. 254, Amer. Literature	3	B
P.E. 103, Phys. Educ.	R	B	Psych. 464, Ind. Psychology	3	B
E.E. 100, Tech. Lecture	R	A	Ec. 365d, Business Law	3	B
Spring, 1939			**Winter, 1949**		
Chem. 102, General Chem.	4	Cxx	Zool. 105, General Biology	3	C
Engl. 103, Freshman Comp.	3	C	Ec. 366, Adv. Business Law	3	C
Math. 103, Anal. Geom.	5	Exx	M.L. 262, Elem. Spanish	3	B
E.Dr. 133, Working Drawing	3	C	Engl. 256, Contemp. Lit.	3	C
P.E. 103, Phys. Educ.	R	B	Ec. 410, Econ. of Ind.Relations	3	C
Lib. 106a, Library Instr.	R	C	Ec. 468, Industrial Marketing	3	C
Spring, 1947			**Spring, 1949**		
Chem. 101, General Chem.	4	A	Zool. 203, Human Biology	3	A
Ec. 261, Prin. of Econ.	3	B	M.L. 263, Elem. Spanish	3	B
Math. 101, College Algebra	5	A	Ec. 263, Prin. of Econ.	3	C
M.E. 204, Metal Fabrication	2	B	Gen.E. 425, Prin. of Pers.Super.	3	X
Summer, 1947			Gen.E. 351, Industrial Organization	3	X
Chem. 102, General Chem.	4	C	Psych. 484, Psych. of Advertising	3	C
Ec. 262, Prin. of Econ.	3	B	**Summer, 1949**		
Gen.E. 105, Engr. Problems	1	B	Ec. 510, Land Use & Conservation	3	B
Math. 102c, Plane Trig.	4	B	M.L. 361, Intermediate Spanish	3	A
M.E. 201, Machine Shop	2	B	M.L. 362, Intermediate Spanish	3	A
Fall, 1947			M.L. 363, Intermediate Spanish	3	A
Chem. 103, Gen. Chem. & Qual. Anal.	4	B	No credit entries valid below this line.		
Psych. 204, General Psych.	3	B	Is Currently Enrolled		
Govt. 315b, Amer.(Meets Cert.Rq.)	3	B	Status: In Good Standing.		
Gen.E. 106, Engr. Problems	1	A			
Math. 103c, Anal. Geom.	4	A			
Winter, 1948					
Math. 211, Calculus	4	C	J. R. Sage,		
E.E. 201, Dir. Current Circuits	5	C	Registrar		
continued in next column.			October 25, 1949		

202

C. Copy of original 7"x 9" V-Mail letter   11/29/1944

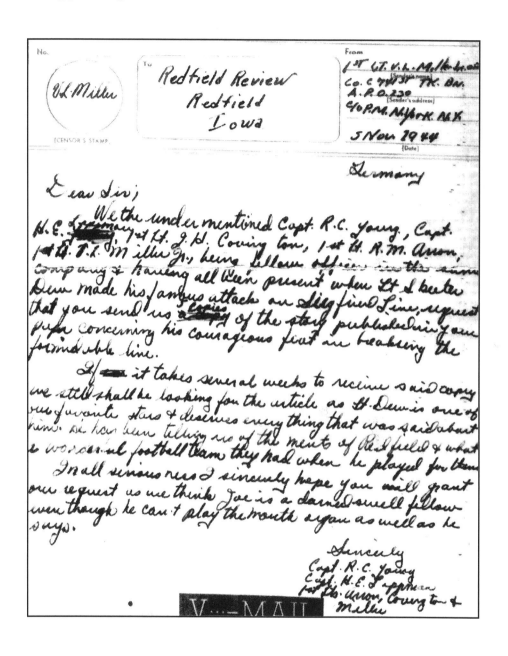

203

D. Ignition Spark Timing Control Patent

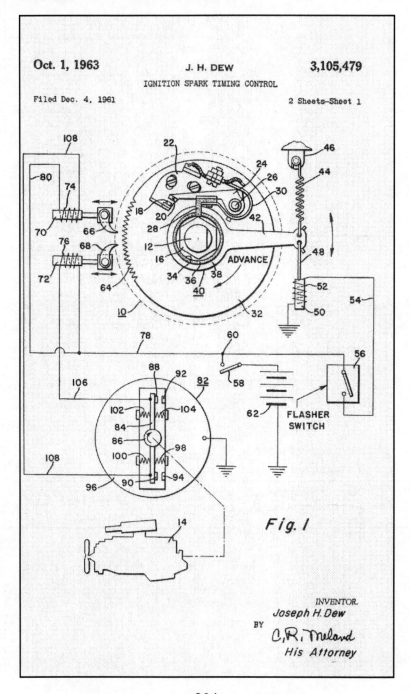

Oct. 1, 1963   J. H. DEW   3,105,479

IGNITION SPARK TIMING CONTROL

Filed Dec. 4, 1961   2 Sheets—Sheet 1

FLASHER SWITCH

ADVANCE

Fig. 1

INVENTOR.
Joseph H. Dew
BY
C. R. Meland
His Attorney

204

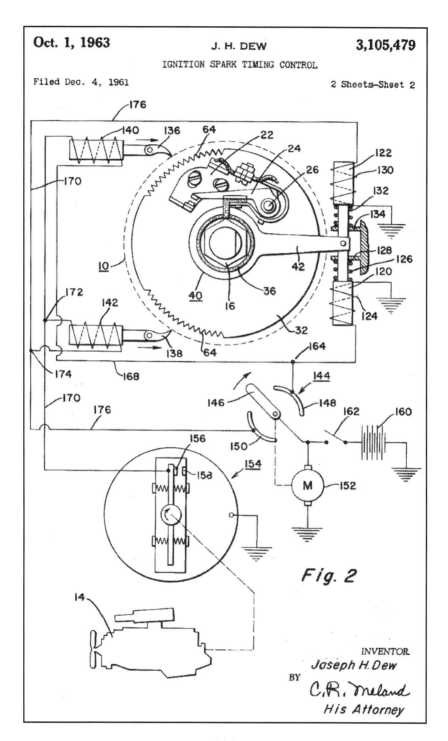

Fig. 2

1

3,105,479
IGNITION SPARK TIMING CONTROL
Joseph H. Dew, Flint, Mich., assignor to General Motors
Corporation, Detroit, Mich., a corporation of Delaware
Filed Dec. 4, 1961, Ser. No. 156,905
12 Claims. (Cl. 123—146.5)

This invention relates to a system for controlling the spark timing of an internal combustion engine and more particularly to a system for controlling the spark advance of the engine distributor in response to changes of speed of the engine.

The amount of acceleration and deceleration of an internal combustion engine depends upon various factors, including, the supply of fuel, gravity, braking and other frictional forces. This acceleration and deceleration also depends on spark setting at a given engine speed and the present invention is directed to a system for automatically adjusting the spark setting of the engine to its optimum value under various conditions of operation.

It accordingly is one of the objects of this invention to provide an ignition timing system for an internal combustion engine wherein changes in speed due to improper spark setting are sensed and the spark setting adjusted to its optimum value in accordance with the information sensed.

Another object of this invention is to provide an ignition system for an internal combustion engine wherein means are provided for constantly varying spark setting together with means for sensing the effect of this variation of spark setting on the engine and for adjusting the spark setting to an optimum condition in accordance with the conditions sensed. In carrying forward this object of the invention, the breaker plate of the distributor is oscillated and this oscillation will cause the engine to accelerate or decelerate. This condition of acceleration or deceleration is sensed and the spark setting is then changed or shifted towards its optimum value.

A further object of this invention is to provide a spark advance arrangement for an engine wherein a rotatable part of the engine distributor that controls spark timing is oscillated over a narrow angle, and further wherein ratchet means are provided under the control of changes in engine speed due to variation of the spark setting for causing the rotatable member to be moved toward an optimum spark setting.

Further objects and advantages of the present invention will be apparent from the following description, reference being had to the accompanying drawings wherein preferred embodiments of the present invention are clearly shown.

In the drawings:

FIGURE 1 is a schematic illustration of an ignition timing control system made in accordance with this invention.

FIGURE 2 is a schematic illustration of a modified ignition control system made in accordance with this invention.

Referring now to the drawings and more particularly to FIGURE 1, the reference numeral 10 designates a distributor for controlling the spark timing of an internal combustion engine. This distributor has the usual shaft 12 which is driven by the internal combustion engine 14. The shaft carrying a conventional cam 16. The cam 16 operates the breaker contacts of the distributor which have been designated by reference numerals 18 and 20. It is seen that the breaker contact 18 is supported by plate member 22 and that breaker contact 20 is carried by a breaker lever 24 which is pivoted to the post 26. The breaker lever 24 has a rubbing block 28 which engages the cam 16 and serves to open the breaker contacts during its rotation. The breaker contacts are normally urged to a closed position by the spring 30.

2

The plate member 22 is carried by a rotatable spark adjusting member 32 and rotation of the member 32 adjusts the rubbing block relative to the breaker cam 16 to control the spark timing for the internal combustion engine 14. Clockwise rotation of the timing plate 32 causes an advance in spark timing whereas counterblockwise rotation of the plate 32 causes the spark to be retarded. The electric circuit for supplying spark impulses to the engine 14 under the control of the opening and closing of breaker contacts 18 and 20 has not been illustrated, it being understood that it is conventional with the breaker points controlling the current flow between a battery and the primary winding of the ignition coil. The distributor 10 may also include the usual rotor and distributor cap for supplying spark impulses to the spark plugs of the engine 14 all of which is well known to those skilled in the art.

The breaker plate or rotatable member 32 has a flange 34 that engages one side of a ring of friction material 36. This friction material also engages the annular portion 38 of an actuating member generally designated by reference numeral 40. The member 40 has an arm 42 formed integral with the annular portion 38 and it will be apparent that as the member 40 is rotated, the member 32 will likewise rotate through engagement with the friction material 36. The fit between the friction material, the flange 34 and the annular member 38 is such that if a force is applied to one of the members to stop its rotation, the other will rotate with respect thereto by slippage on the friction material.

The arm member 42 has one end thereof connected with a spring 44 which is secured to the fixed member 46. The arm member 42 is also connected with a rod 48 which is shifted by the armature 50 of an electromagnetic actuator that includes the coil winding 52. The coil winding 52 has one side thereof connected with lead wire 54 and it is seen that this lead wire is connected to one side of a rapidly cycling flasher switch 56 which opens and closes at a rapid rate when energized. The flasher switch should be designed so that its closing time is greater than the time that it is open so that coil 52 is energized for a longer period than it is deenergized during one cycle of operation of the switch 56. The switch may cycle, for example 60 times per minute and it is apparent to those skilled in the art that this switch could be of a type other than a thermal switch as long as its closing time is of longer duration than its open time.

The opposite side of the flasher switch 56 is connected to junction 60. The junction 60 is connected to one side of a battery 62 through ignition switch 58. The opposite side of the battery is connected directly to ground.

It will be apparent that when the switch 58 is closed, the flasher switch is energized to periodically open and close and therefore periodically energize the coil winding 52 at a rapid rate. As noted above, the coil winding 52 will be energized for a longer period than when it is deenergized over one cycle of operation of the switch 56. When the coil winding 52 is energized, the arm 42 will be shifted clockwise to advance the spark setting and when the coil winding is deenergized, the spring 44 will pull the arm 42 counterclockwise. In this manner, the arm 42 will be oscillated over a narrow angle from its position shown on the drawing to a position which is clockwise of the position shown on the drawing.

The rotatable timing plate 32 is formed with a plurality of ratchet teeth 64 formed along its circumference. The spacing between the ratchet teeth may be, for example, .25°. These ratchet teeth cooperate with the pawls 66 and 68 which are operated respectively by the armatures 70 and 72 of solenoids which include the coil windings 74 and

3

76. It can be seen that one side of the coil winding 76 is connected to one side of the battery 62 via the lead wire 78 and the junction 60. One side of the coil winding 74 is likewise connected to one side of the battery 62 via the lead wire 80.

The spark advance system of this invention includes a sensing device which is generally designated by reference numeral 82. This sensing device comprises a switch actuator 84 which is driven by a shaft 86. The switch actuator 84 has contacts 88 and 90 which cooperate with contacts 92 and 94 carried by a flywheel 96. The flywheel 96 is connected to the switch actuator 84 by the springs 98, 100, 102 and 104. The shaft 86 is driven by the engine 14 as is clearly apparent from FIGURE 1. The contacts 92 and 94 are connected directly to ground as through the flywheel or through any other conventional arrangement.

It will be apparent that when the engine 14 is accelerating and the shaft 86 rotating in the direction indicated by the arrow, the contacts 88 and 92 will close. On the other hand, when the engine 14 is decelerating, the contacts 90 and 94 close and the contacts 88 and 92 remain open. When there is no acceleration or deceleration, both pairs of contacts 88 and 92 and 90 and 94 remain in an open position.

It can be seen that the contact actuator 84 is connected to one side of the solenoid coil winding 76 via lead wire 106 and is also connected to one side of coil winding 74 via the lead wire 108. It will, of course, be appreciated that contacts 88 and 90 may be insulated from each other and that lead wire 106 could be connected directly with contact 88 with the lead wire 108 being directly connected with contact 90. One end of the springs connected between the contact actuator 84 and the flywheel 96 are insulated so that there is no electrical connection between the contact actuator 84 and ground except when the contacts 88 and 92 or 90 and 94 are in engagement.

In operation of the ignition timing control apparatus of this invention, the manually operable switch 58 is closed when it is desired to run the engine. When switch 58 is closed, the switch 56 opens and closes to cause the arm 42 to be oscillated through a small angle. When the coil winding 52 is energized, the arm 42 will be moved in a clockwise direction and carries the plate member 32 with it so that the plate member is moved in a clockwise direction. This movement of the plate member 32 will cause an advance in spark setting. This advance in spark setting will move the plate 32 either towards or away from its optimum spark setting for a given engine speed. If this movement is toward the optimum spark setting, the engine will be accelerated whereas if this movement is away from the optimum spark setting, the engine will decelerate.

If it is assumed that the clockwise movement of arm 42 has advanced the plate 32 towards its optimum setting, the engine accelerates. When the engine accelerates, the contacts 88 and 92 will close and the coil winding 76 will be energized to force the pawl member 68 into engagement with the ratchet teeth 64. The pawl member 68 and the ratchet teeth 64 are designed to provide ratcheting when the rotatable member 32 is moving clockwise but to prevent movement of the rotatable member 32 if it is urged in a counterclockwise direction. It thus can be seen that when the arm 42 moves in a clockwise direction, it will carry the member 32 with it and the pawl member 68 will ratchet over the ratchet teeth 64. As the coil winding 52 becomes deenergized, the pawl member 68 prevents the member 32 from following the movement of the arm 42 in a counterclockwise direction due to slippage on the friction material 36. It thus is seen that if the plate 32 is shifted clockwise and causes an acceleration of the engine due to the forced change in spark setting, the pawl 68 will be projected to cause a slight adjustment of the timing plate 32 in the clockwise direction and therefore towards optimum spark setting.

If a clockwise movement of the timing plate 32 causes a

4

deceleration of the engine, it indicates that the timing plate is being moved away from its optimum spark setting position. Assuming that the timing plate is moving away from its optimum spark setting for a given speed, the engine is then decelerated and the contacts 90 and 94 will close. This causes the solenoid coil winding 74 to be energized and causes the pawl 66 to be moved into engagement with the ratchet teeth 64. The pawl 66 and the ratchet teeth 64 are so arranged that during counterclockwise movement of plate 32, the pawl 66 ratchets over the teeth 64. During clockwise movement of the plate 32, the pawl 66 will become engaged with one of the teeth 64 to prevent further clockwise rotation of the plate 32. It thus is seen that during deceleration when the contacts 90 and 94 are closed, the pawl 66 will stop clockwise movement of the plate 32 and the arm 42 and therefore shift relative to the plate 32. When solenoid coil winding 52 then becomes deenergized, the arm 42 and the plate 32 will move counterclockwise together thus shifting the plate a slight amount in a direction to retard the spark which now is in a direction towards the optimum spark setting for the operating conditions of the engine.

It can be seen from the foregoing that the plate 32 is intentionally advanced and the results of this advance on engine operation is sensed and a connection then made to shift the plate towards its optimum spark setting. Thus, if an acceleration of the engine occurs upon an advance of the plate 32, it indicates that the plate is moving towards its optimum spark setting and the sensing device 82 therefore causes the plate to be shifted clockwise toward its optimum spark setting. On the other hand, if an advance of the plate 32 causes the engine to decelerate, this condition is sensed by the sensing device 82 and is translated into a retarding movement or counterclockwise movement of the plate 32.

In the system of FIGURE 1, the timing plate 32 has its adjustment controlled solely by reciprocations of arm 42. The device illustrated in FIGURE 1 is fully capable of controlling spark timing but it will be apparent to those skilled in the art that it also could be used as a fine adjustment control for distributors that have the conventional vacuum and centrifugal advance controls. If desired, a stop may be provided to limit the range of spark advance to that which the engine requires.

Referring now more particularly to FIGURE 2, a modified ignition timing control system is illustrated which is similar in many respects to that of FIGURE 1. The FIGURE 2 system is simpler than the one illustrated in FIGURE 1 and is immune to shifting of the breaker plate or timing plate in response to gravity, supply of fuel, braking or other frictional causes. It is sensitive to acceleration caused by a change in spark setting. In FIGURE 2, the same reference numerals have been used as were used in FIGURE 1 to identify corresponding parts in each figure.

In FIGURE 2, the arm 42 is connected with armatures 120 and 122. The armature 120 and the coil winding 124 form part of a solenoid actuator which when energized moves the arm 42 in a clockwise direction. A compression spring 126 is positioned between the armature 120 and a fixed abutment 128 to shift the arm 42 to a neutral position when the solenoid coil winding 124 is deenergized. In a similar fashion, the armature 122 and coil winding 130 form a solenoid actuator for moving the arm 42 in a counterclockwise direction. A compression spring 132 is positioned between the armature 122 and a fixed abutment 134. It can be seen that when neither coil winding 130 nor coil winding 124 is energized, the springs 126 and 132 move the arm 42 to a neutral position. Energization of coil winding 130 shifts the arm 42 in a counterclockwise direction to retard the spark whereas energization of coil winding 124 shifts the arm 42 in a clockwise direction to advance the spark.

The timing plate 32 once more has ratchet teeth 64 which cooperate respectively with pawls 136 and 138.

E. Method and Apparatus for Separating Sheet Materials Patent

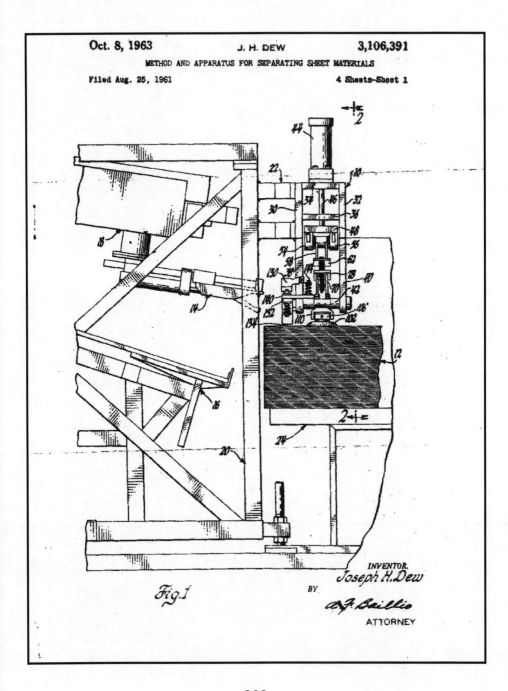

Fig.1

INVENTOR.
Joseph H. Dew

BY

ATTORNEY

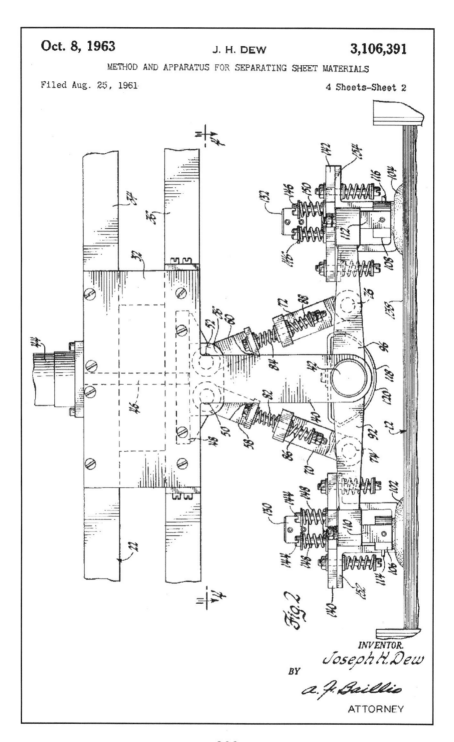

Fig. 2

INVENTOR.

Joseph H. Dew

BY

a. F. Baillio

ATTORNEY

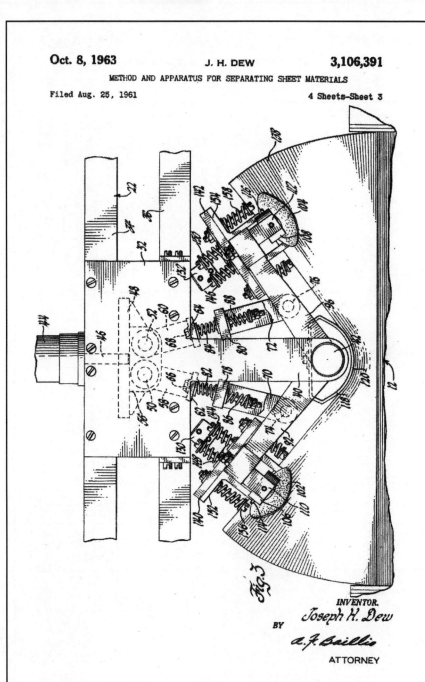

Fig.3

INVENTOR.

Joseph H. Dew

BY

A. F. Baillio

ATTORNEY

210

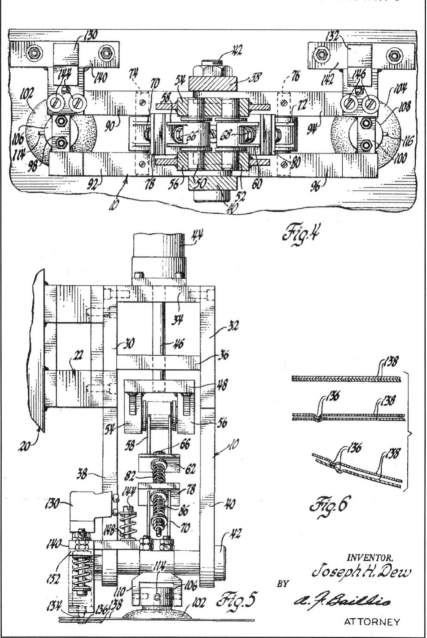

Fig.4

Fig.5

Fig.6

INVENTOR.
Joseph H. Dew
BY
a. f. Baillio
ATTORNEY

1

3,106,391
METHOD AND APPARATUS FOR SEPARATING
SHEET MATERIALS
Joseph H. Dew, Flint, Mich., assignor to General Motors
Corporation, Detroit, Mich., a corporation of Dela-
ware
Filed Aug. 25, 1961, Ser. No. 134,012
6 Claims. (Cl. 271—27)

This invention relates to a method and apparatus for separating sheet materials and more particularly to a method and apparatus for separating stacked steel plates which are heavily lubricated prior to a metal forming operation.

In modern automated metal working operations where-in large metallic sheets of steel or the like are formed by bending operations in large presses, automatic means are conventionally provided to remove a single sheet of material from a supply stack adjacent the press and to transfer the sheet of material into position within the press. In order to maintain high rates of production, means must be provided to separate single sheets from the supply stack in a minimum amount of time and with unerring accuracy. The difficulties involved in separation of sheets of material which are stored in vertical stacks are well known. In metal forming operations of large parts, such as automobile body panels, the metallic blanks are heavily lubricated and, consequently, the problem of separating stacked sheets is multiplied many fold. The use of vacuum cups which are adapted to engage and remove the top sheet from a stack of sheets is a well known expedient. Although vacuum cups can successfully grip the top sheet of a stack of sheets, additional means have been required to separate the next adjacent sheets from the top sheet to facilitate rapid sheet separation and insure that only one sheet is removed at one time. In previous practice, such devices as high pressure air blasts and magnetic separating means have commonly been utilized. In spite of many previous suggestions, the separation of stacked sheets still remains a production limiting problem.

The purpose of this invention is to provide a new and improved sheet separating method and apparatus for removing the top sheet from a stack of sheets with improved speed and accuracy. Another purpose of this invention is to provide sheet separating means of simplified construction and utilizing a minimum number of parts. Still another purpose of this invention is to utilize conventional vacuum cup clamping devices in a more efficient manner. Other objects and advantages of the present invention are disclosed in the following detailed description wherein an illustrative embodiment of the present invention is described by reference to the accompanying drawings wherein:

FIGURE 1 is a side elevational view of apparatus embodying the present invention;

FIGURE 2 is a partial elevational view taken along the line 2—2 in FIGURE 1;

FIGURE 3 is an illustration of the apparatus shown in FIGURE 2 in an operating position;

FIGURE 4 is a sectional view taken along the line 4—4 in FIGURE 2;

FIGURE 5 is an enlarged partial view of the sheet separating apparatus shown in FIGURE 1; and

FIGURE 6 is a sequential illustration of the separation of stacked sheets with the present invention.

Referring now to FIGURE 1, the present invention relates to an improved sheet separating mechanism designated generally at 10 which is adapted to remove the top sheet from a stack of sheets 12 so that a conventional mechanical hand 14 can grip the displaced top sheet and

2

move it onto a conventional sheet feeding mechanism 16 for delivery to a press. The mechanical hand 14 is supported by conventional positioning apparatus 18 which allows the sheet of material to be completely removed from the supply stack 12 and correctly positioned on the conveyor means 16. The mechanical hand and the conveyor means are mounted within a frame 20 to which the sheet separator 10 may be fixed by suitable braces 22 and located in alignment above the supply stack 12. The stack of sheets 12 is supported on a conventional table 24 having hydraulically actuated vertical adjustment means to maintain the top of the supply stack at substantially the same level at all times.

The apparatus is controlled by conventional circuitry in a conventional manner. The general sequence of operation is initiated by energization of a valve which causes air to flow past a venturi system located at the center of the vacuum cups to create a vacuum in a conventional manner. A second valve is thereafter energized to cause the vacuum cups to be extended into engagement with the top sheet of the supply stack. The second valve is then de-energized to cause the vacuum cups to be retracted and to simultaneously remove the top sheet from the supply stack. At this time, an electrical signal is generated to cause the iron hand to be extended and to clamp onto the separated upper sheet. Another electrical signal then shuts off the airflow to the venturi system to eliminate the vacuum and release the cups from the top sheet. At this time, the iron hand control 18 is energized to remove the sheet of material form the supply stack 12 and position it on the sheet feeding means 16.

Referring now to FIGURES 2–5, the sheet separating mechanism 10 comprises a frame formed from parallelly spaced side plates 30, 32 which are connected by spaced cross plates 34, 36. The side plates are T-shaped and have downwardly extending support arms 38, 40 which are connected at their lower ends by a pin element 42. A power cylinder 44 is fixedly secured to the cross plate 34 and has a reciprocable piston rod 46 extending downwardly therefrom. The end of the piston rod is fixedly secured to a connecting block 48 having a pair of horizontal pin elements 50, 52 supported between depending flanges 54, 56. Upper control link elements 58, 60 are rotatably mounted on the pin elements 50, 52, respectively. Each of the upper control link elements terminates in transversely extending flange portions 62, 64 through which connecting bolts or the like 66, 68 extend. Lower control link elements 70, 72 are pivotally secured at the lower ends to pin elements 74, 76 and are provided with transversely extending flange portions 78, 80 at the upper ends. The bolts 66, 68 extend through the flange portions 78, 80 and are fixedly located relative thereto by means of compression springs 82, 84 and 86, 88. The compression springs floatatively suport the lower control link elements relative to the upper control link elements and allow limited relative movement therebetween.

Referring now particularly to FIGURE 4, a pair of oppositely extending vacuum cup lift arms are formed by spaced parallelly extending members 90, 92 and 94, 96, respectively. The inner ends of each of the members are pivotally mounted on the pin element 42 and the outer ends are connected by cross braces 98, 100. Referring now to FIGURE 5, conventional vacuum cups 102, 104 having vacuum forming suuport heads 106, 108 are pivotally connected to bifurcated support brackets 110, 112 which are secured to the cross braces 98, 100. Each of the vacuum cups is connected by conduits 114, 116 to vacuum producing means in a conventional manner. A sheet engaging and bending control shoe 118 is mounted on the pin element 42 between the spaced members 90, 92 and 94, 96. The lower surface 120 of the bending shoe is provided with a curved surface adapted to support

212

3

the area of bend of the sheet being transferred. The shoe is pivotally mounted and is, therefore, self-centering relative to the sheet being lifted. The shoe is provided with a contact surface of sufficient length and having a large enough radius of curvature to insure sufficient support for the sheet being lifted in the bend area and to permit maximum flexure of the sheet being lifted without deformation thereof.

In order to insure that only one sheet at a time will be removed from the supply stack, special apparatus is provided to cause initial separation of the top sheet from the next adjacent sheet and to further provide a positive wedge-like action between the top sheet and the next adjacent sheet as the top sheet is flexed by the lift mechanism. The special apparatus comprises a pair of conventional pneumatic hammers 130, 132 which are connected in a conventional manner by flexible conduits to a power source. As shown in FIGURE 5, each of the pneumatic hammers is provided with a reciprocable tool 134 which is adapted to form indentations 136 in the top sheet 138 of the supply stack for a purpose to be hereinafter described. Each of the pneumatic hammers is mounted on support brackets 140, 142 which are floatively secured to the members 90, 94 by bolts 144, 146 and compression springs 148, 150. The compression springs 148, 150 permit limited movement of the support brackets 140, 142 relative to the lift arms to compensate for variations in location of the top sheet of the supply stack and to allow the vacuum cups 102, 104 to be firmly positioned against the top sheet regardless of such variations. Each of the pneumatic hammers is additionally supported in U-shaped guide brackets 152, 154 which are secured to the brackets 140, 142, respectively, by similar bolt and compression spring arrangements 156, 158 which permit limited relative movement of the brackets 152, 154 relative to the support plates 140, 142 to provide additional means to maintain flexibility of the pneumatic hammers relative to the vacuum cups.

Operation

In operation and at the beginning of a sheet separation cycle, the lift mechanism is in the position illustrated in FIGURE 3 with the vacuum cups 102, 104 deactivated and no sheet secured thereon. At the proper time, in relation to press cycle and the sheet feeding sequence from the conveyor 16, the cylinder 44 is actuated to downwardly extend the piston rod 46 and connecting block 48, and thereby rotate the lift arms into a substantially horizontal position by pivotal movement about the pin means 42. The vacuum forming means connected to the vacuum cups through the conduits 114, 116 are simultaneously actuated so that the vacuum cups will grippingly engage the upper surface of the top sheet of the supply stack which is maintained at a constant height by the hydraulic table. The bolt and spring connections, which support the pneumatic hammers 130, 132 relative to the lift arms, permit the lower surface of the reciprocable tool 134 to be located in surface engagement with the top sheet without interfering with the action of the vacuum cups. When the lift mechanism has been fully extended, the pneumatic hammers 130, 132 are actuated to drive the hammer tips into the top sheet and form an indentation therein as shown at 136 in FIGURES 5 and 6. The hammers are located outwardly of the vacuum cups along a portion of the sheets which is subsequently trimmed so that the indentations in no way blemish the finished product. As shown in FIGURE 6, actuation of the pneumatic hammers and formation of the indentations 136 cause an initial separation of the top sheet from the next adjacent sheet. After the pneumatic hammers have been actuated, the cylinder 44 is actuated to cause retraction of the piston rod 46, the connecting block 48, and the lift links so that the lift arms are pivoted upwardly about the pin means 42. The vacuum cups are securely gripped on the upper surface of the top sheet

4

and lift and flex the upper sheet as illustrated in FIGURE 3. During the first portion of the upward movement, the indentations in the top sheet are horizontally displaced relative to the next adjacent sheet to provide a positive wedging action therebetween as shown in FIGURE 6. This is because the surface attraction between adjacent sheets will cause the next adjacent sheet to momentarily hang onto the top sheet as it is lifted and flexed. However, since the top sheet is being flexed about a shorter radius than the next adjacent sheet, there will be a sliding action between the top surface of the next adjacent sheet and the bottom surface of the top sheet. This sliding action causes a horizontal displacement of the indentations 36 producing the wedging action. This action is particularly useful when the sheets are oily and have a much greater surface attraction than if they were dry. Continued upward movement of the lift arms increases the pivotal displacement of the vacuum cups from the original substantially horizontal position and flexes the top sheet about the shoe 120. When the lift arm has been fully retracted, the iron hand 14 clamps the adjacent edge of the top sheet and the vacuum in cups 102, 104 is dissipated so that the sheet may be removed by the iron hand.

The present apparatus has several advantages and specific areas of improvement over the prior art which should be noted. A comparison of the subject apparatus with prior apparatus will show that a substantial simplification and reduction in the number of parts required for successful separation of stacked sheets has been attained. Only one operating cylinder is required and a plurality of vacuum cups are operated thereby. In the prior art, blank separators commonly used independent air cylinders for each of the vacuum cups utilized. Furthermore, the attainable degree of flexing of the top sheet to obtain complete disassociation from the next adjacent sheets has been greatly increased by the present apparatus. The provision of a common pivotal axis for the pivotally mounted lift arms permits flexing of the sheet to a degree heretofore unknown. It is apparent that the greater the flexure of the top sheet, the more readily the top sheet is disassociated from the next adjacent sheets. Furthermore, in prior art devices, the vacuum cup lift mechanisms were arranged in a manner such that a sliding action of the vacuum cups relative to the surface of the sheet being lifted was encountered during the separating operation. In the present apparatus, there is no sliding of the sheet being separated relative to the vacuum cups because of the special design of the lift mechanism. With the present apparatus, the sheets to be separated can be flexed to their elastic limit to facilitate separation of adjacent sheets. It is even contemplated that in some instances the sheets may be flexed beyond their elastic limit, if necessary, to obtain satisfactory separation of the sheet when a slight deformation in the sheets will not affect the finished product.

The provision of the pneumatic hammers, which are integrally associated with the lift arms and produce a new cooperative result in combination therewith, is a most important feature of the invention. The pneumatic hammers are mounted in a manner to eliminate any interference with the function of the vacuum cups 102, 104. By providing indentations in the top sheet, a positive wedging separation of the top sheet from the next adjacent sheet is obtained as the lift arms are retracted and the sheet is initially flexed. In dealing with heavily lubricated sheets, the positive wedging action breaks the lubricant film between the top sheet and the next adjacent sheet so that the sheets may be more readily separated. Those skilled in the art will readily appreciate the difficulties encountered in separating heavily lubricated sheets and the importance of breaking the lubricant film so that the sheet adjacent the top sheet is not carried upwardly when the upper sheet is removed by the vacuum cups.

5

It is to be understood that the aforedescribed apparatus is merely illustrative in many of the details of construction and the arrangements of the various parts. Insofar as the advantages of the present invention can be obtained by obvious modifications, such modifications are intended to be included within the scope of the appended claims, except insofar as limited by the prior art.

I claim:

1. Means for separating sheet material comprising a pair of oppositely extending lift arms, said lift arms being mounted on a common axis, constituting a stationary pivot, sheet gripping means provided on the ends of said lift arms, a single actuating means for pivotally moving said lift arms about said common axis from a first position of engagement with the top of a sheet of material supported on a stack of sheets to a second position pivotally displaced toward one another whereat the sheet is separated from the stack of sheets, and control linkage interconnecting said actuating means and said lift arms to positively displace said lift arms between said positions.

2. In apparatus for separating the top sheet from a stack of sheets, a pair of pivotally mounted oppositely extending lift arms, said lift arms being pivoted about a common axis for movement between a first position substantially parallel to said stack of sheets and a second position pivotally inclined toward one another and relative to said stack of sheets, vacuum cup means associated with each of said lift arms to engage and lift sheets from said stack of sheets, a single power cylinder to simultaneously actuate said lift arms between said positions, control linkage extending between said power cylinder and said lift arms, pneumatic hammers secured to and carried by said arms, and said pneumatic hammers having means to form indentations in the top sheet prior to movement of said lift arms from said second position to said first position to provide a positive wedging action between the top sheet and the next adjacent sheet of the stack of sheets as said lift arms are moved from said first position to said second position.

3. The apparatus as defined in claim 2 and wherein said pneumatic hammers are connected to said lift arms

6

by cushioning means which permit limited relative displacement of the pneumatic hammers relative to the lifting arms to eliminate interference of the pneumatic hammers with the operation of said vacuum cups.

4. The apparatus as defined in claim 2 and wherein shoe means are mounted coaxially with said lift arms to engage said sheet and control flexure thereof during movement of said lift arms from said first position to said second position.

5. The apparatus as defined in claim 2 and wherein said link means includes lost motion spring connections to compensate for variations in the amount of pivotal movement of said lift arms needed to obtain a predetermined amount of flexure in said sheet.

6. The method of removing the top sheet from a stack of sheets, said sheets characterized by being permanently locally deformable when a localized impact force is applied thereto and comprising the steps of: striking the top sheet on the upper surface thereof with a deforming tool so as to produce a localized deformation therein, said localized deformation being of sufficient penetration to also deform the bottom surface of said top sheet thereby locally separating same from the next adjacent sheet, flexing said top sheet and necessarily the next adjacent sheet when the surface attraction therebetween is sufficient to cause them to hang together and sliding the localized deformation of the top sheet relative to the next adjacent sheet causing a positive wedging action between the top sheet and the next adjacent sheet by horizontal displacement of the deformation relative to the next adjacent sheet, and removing said top sheet from the stack without removing the next adjacent sheet.

References Cited in the file of this patent
UNITED STATES PATENTS

853,910	Tyden	_____	May 14, 1907
1,911,884	Darbaker	_____	May 30, 1933
2,406,766	Harrold	_____	Sept. 3, 1946
2,941,799	Reincke	_____	June 21, 1960
3,033,562	Dretz	_____	May 8, 1962

F. Evelyn Johnston Family

Evelyn's parents came from Argenta, Illinois in a covered wagon in the early 1900s. W.T. worked in a brewery and was a brick mason when a young man. Later, he was a successful farmer and had a sorghum mill near Stuart, Iowa.

Willis T. Johnson	and	Eudora Clifton Johnson
09/19/1871 - 09/15/1944		10/23/1879 – 1/22/1953

Ola Jane (Thompson)	08/12/1896	-02/03/1934
Leroy James Johnson	04/09/1898	- 03/31/ 1899
Hazel Marie (Mobley/Arrasmith)	01/11/1900	- 04/01/1978
Carl Milton Johnson	12/06/1901	- 08/22/1973
Earl Earnest Johnson	10/01/1903	- 03/03/1945
Mary <u>Gladys</u> (Conant)	11/18/1905	- 11/16/1996
Wava <u>Grace</u> (Gilliland) (King)	10/28/1906	- 08/08/19-64
Donald Edwin Johnson	11/15/1908	- 11/22/1973
Clarence Matthew Johnston*	01/8/1911	-06/24/1990
Martha Mae (Countryman)	06/20/1913	- 05/20/2005
Dortha Vivian (Stapes)	04/02/1915	- 07/14/2004
Willis Theodore Johnston*	03/17/1918	- 07/20/2001
Evelyn Roine (Dew)	02/14/1922	- 09/03/1990

* Clarence (Pete) and Willis discovered their family name originally was Johnston and had their names legally changed.

Leroy   **Ola**   **Carl**

215

Grace, Dortha, Martha, Hazel, Evelyn, Gladys 1961

Don, Willis, Carl, Clarence 1961

216

Evelyn Roine Johnston Dew

Evelyn Johnston, age 17 youngest of 13

I was a Valentine's day baby, born February 14 in Guthrie County along Middle Raccoon River near Dexter, Iowa. My folks lived on the Cathcart farm for 23 years. I was the youngest of 13 children. I

217

grew up with lots of nieces and nephews my age roaming the woods and river.

At age five, I started school as a first grader at Pioneer School. We walked the mile and a quarter to and from school. Miss Martha Stringham was my favorite teacher through grammar school. I graduated from the 8th grade in the spring of 1935 and started high school in the fall at Redfield, graduating in 1939.

One day our daughter, Elaine, asked, "Mom, how was life when you were a little girl?" Dreaming of the old days was a romantic dream for her. But I'm sure she would have found less romance in everyday living then than now. Things were just more basic then.

Eudora Christa Clifton Johnson and William Thomas Johnson

Our family was a close-knit family, headed by Mom and Dad. I always thought of them as a unit, yet each had their own personality and strength. Dad whose full name was William Thomas Johnson, known as W.T., was born September 29, 1871. He was six feet tall, lean, with brown eyes. He had curly brown hair when he was a young man. He was quite distinguished looking, which must have come from his English ancestry, although there were some French and Indian bloods mixed. (*Ancestors go back to a French trapper named D'Sprague who married Namequa, the daughter of Blackhawk, war chief of the Sauk and Fox.*) When I knew my dad, he was bald, slim, and wore a full-trim mustache. The girls at the dances would tweak his mustache making Mom very jealous. Dad was one of those strong, silent gentlemen. My son Dennis reminds me of him in both manner and build. He never talked ill of anyone. He always said, "Never talk about anyone unless you can say something good." He was always there to discuss your problems and offer a solution. Then he expected you to act on it or on one of your own.

Dad's only vice (I never thought of it as such) was chewing tobacco. I can still see him sitting by the dining room table with his dime-store glasses on, reading the paper, and chewing. He always tore a small corner off the paper to use as a blind on his glasses to keep the light from the kerosene lamp from shining in his eyes. Those lamps never seemed that bright to me! Occasionally, he would lean to the left and a shot of brown liquid would hit the tin can he used for a spittoon. He never missed. Oh woe to the child who in a spurt of energy ran around the table and kicked the can over. Of course, you had to clean it up---no paper towels in those days. Rags? Yes, but we wore those. A few corncobs and a dustpan got the worst, then a bucket of soapy water finished the floor and dustpan. One gave Dad and chair a wide berth until memory faded.

Dad was a stern father. He never spanked me, no need. Just speaking my name in that deep voice of his was enough to straighten me up. He was a fair and just father and I loved him.

How can one describe one's mother? One can say she was born in 1879. She was christened Eudora Christa Clifton. She was five feet tall, weighed 98 pounds when she married Dad at age 16, January 1, 1896. Dad was 24 when they married. She had dark, straight hair, and devilish, brown eyes. But she was much more than that. Mom loved life and was full of it. She was the soul of wisdom, love, tenderness, and gaiety.

Clifton Sisters: Back Anna, Martha, Eudora Front-Minnie, Sarah

Eudora's parents
Joseph S. and Mary Ann Clifton

WT's Grandmother
Naomi Cook
Her husband Joseph Sprague was
son of Namequa , Black Hawk's daughter

Mom loved children, as did Dad. They had thirteen children, I was the youngest. Ola, LeRoy, Hazel, Carl, Earl, Grace and Martha went by Johnson. Gladys, Donald, Clarence, Dortha, Willis, and Evelyn by Johnston. (*There is a discrepancy on this since Evelyn's birth certificate says Johnson.*) Everyone used to say to me "13 how unlucky!" But I always felt lucky to be born and loved. Having lots of brothers and sisters wasn't all bad. Some of my older brothers and sisters were married and had children before I was born. Even though we lived in the country, I had lots of playmates near my age.

Nephew Keith Thompson with Aunt Evelyn
At river bottom farm
3088 Zack Lane,
Redfield, IA 50233

Keith and Evelyn

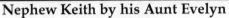

Nephew Keith by his Aunt Evelyn   Evelyn in barrel on farm

Mom knew how and when to punish a child for his wrongdoings. In fact, I got by with very little. She could read me like a book and I'm sure she had eyes in the back of her head. If I lied to her (and I tried a few times), she would just look at me and wait. She knew it wouldn't be long until I broke and told the truth. She was "all wise" until I was about fourteen, then her advice and remarks were up for questioning. But it didn't take many years to discover she was right 98% of the time.

Mom tried to make the punishment fit the crime. One time my brother Carl was playing with his glass of milk. Mom warned him, but to no avail. Over went the milk. She made him lap it off the oilcloth like a kitten. Hazel my sister thought it would be smart to push his nose into the milk. Soon there were two lapping milk.

Mom did not believe in sparing the rod and spoiling the child. Many a time, one would see a child lying face down across her lap getting a "lickin."

Mom was never just resting, sitting still, or idling. If and when she sat down in her favorite chair, an oak rocker, she picked up mending, darning, or crocheting from a pile beside her chair. All our quilts were handmade as well as our dresses and coats, also our underwear. We called them bloomers in those days. She crocheted

222

every son and daughter a tablecloth, bedspread, or made them an appliquéd quilt.

I got my first store-bought coat the winter I was in the eighth grade. It was a navy blue wool chinchilla, well, not really. Since I would be a freshman attending Redfield High School the following fall, it was bought large enough for me to "grow into." Evidently, I had my growth, because I never did "grow into" it.

Mom was the neighborhood nurse. She had a gentle touch with ill or injured. I remember her delivering the neighbor's baby. When the doctor finally arrived several hours later, Mom was furious because he charged full price for delivery and he hadn't done a thing. When as children we would get up in the morning sick, hoping for a day off from school, she always asked what we were sick for. I always wanted coffee. She would fix a cup of rich milk, flavor it with coffee, serve it with crackers, and soon I was off to school. We were discouraged from drinking coffee by being told it would turn us black. But it didn't work. We were also told that eating fat would curl your hair. Guess I never ate enough.

Mom nursed us through all those childhood diseases one seldom hears of today. We had German measles, measles, scarlet fever, chicken pox, whooping cough, diphtheria, mumps, and the usual number of colds. Plus, all the breaks and sprains an active child incurs.

One of my most painful injuries was stepping on a nail barefooted. I can still hear the flesh tear as the nail pierced the sole of my foot. I shudder yet. Mom would work the wound to make it bleed and then soak it in iodine. I hopped around on one foot until it healed, then off for more adventure.

A cow-witch is a painful thing, too. A cow-witch is a slit on the underside of the joint of a toe. We would smear a piece of yarn with lard and tie it around the toe.

I remember once when someone brought the "itch" to school. Mom got out the sulfur. She mixed it with lard to rub on the rash and mixed it with molasses to take internally. Lordy, how that stuff can itch!!! It was always a very embarrassing and shameful thing to have.

Mom was always there when we needed her. I loved her dearly. She was loved by all and made life fun. She put a new meaning to the word "MOM."

Dad and Mom were born, raised, and married in Illinois. They moved to the Cathcart farm on Middle Raccoon River located six miles northwest of Dexter, Iowa in 1920. Although Dad preferred doing masonry work, he figured farming was the best way to make a living with all the children he had. And what a better way to keep them busy. I was the last born. Dad was 50 years old and mom was 42. Mom must have thought her childbearing years would never end.

Living on the rich bottomland near the river, we were known as "River Rats" or "Hayseeds." We had many exciting times with that river, especially when the heavy rains came and the river rose out of its banks. The livestock had to be brought to higher ground and the farm machinery pulled up out of its reach. Sometimes, if the river rose while we were at school, dad would hitch the team to the wagon and come get us. Then we'd race the river home. You see we lived on the other side. Dad was a Knight in Shining Armor, standing braced with his legs apart at the front of the wagon, holding the reins, urging the horses onward. We always won.

The river provided many hours of happiness for us kids. We waded, swam, fished, and explored its banks and bottom. We had a grapevine swing that we swung out over the water and dropped in. My brother Donald found a prehistoric bison head in the soapstone riverbank. The head is now on display in the Historical Building in Des Moines, Iowa.

One time, Dad was plowing on the Allis-Chalmers tractor. He either went to sleep or failed to turn quickly enough and ran off a 20-foot bank into the river. Luckily, he wasn't hurt.

Mom always raised the garden. Dad plowed and harrowed the ground, and then Mom took over. We always had a huge garden with potatoes, corn, beans, tomatoes, cucumbers, radishes, onions, and greens. We canned or stored most of our winter's food, even our meats. Chickens were left on the hoof until the day of eating. It was the best way of preserving them, unless the weasels or mink beat you to them. One time we heard a commotion in the henhouse. Mom went out and found 50 dead chickens, all with their throats cut.

Late in the fall, when the temperature had cooled considerably, Dad would butcher several hogs and a beef. Butchering day was always exciting. The day before, Dad whetted the knives to a razor's sharp edge. Wood was brought to the butchering site and a fire laid, ready to be lit under a barrel of water. Dad lit the fire early butchering day to heat the barrel of water for scalding. Only hogs were scalded, beef were skinned. The beef hide was sold. When all was ready, Dad would shoot the hog between the eyes, slit its throat, and hang it to bleed before dipping it into hot water to scald the hair for easy removal.

Then the hog was scraped until it was clean and white. Even the black and red hogs were white when scraped. When the hog was all scraped and gutted, it was left hanging all night to cool. It was hung high to prevent animals from getting to it.

The liver, heart, and other goodies were brought to the kitchen for Mom to start working on. Fresh liver for supper was a certainty. We had a huge iron kettle in the washhouse that we used for rendering lard, making souse, headcheese, and Pannhaas.

Mom made a variety of recipes, some better than others. Pork Souse was souse made with the ears, feet, knuckles and shoulder part of a pig. Souse was made by fully cooking the meat and then marinating it for a long time in a solution made of fresh lime or lemon juice, vinegar, salt, parsley, minced hot pepper, and cucumbers. Headcheese was a jellied loaf made from chopped and boiled parts of the feet, head, and sometimes the tongue and heart of a hog. Pannhaas was a form of scrapple, all the stuff left over from hogs after butchering, mixed with jellied lard and cornmeal flour.

The sausage was made into patties or put in casings, then fried down. It was then stored in large crocks in lard. Covered and placed in the cellar, it kept for some time. Hams and bacon were cured and smoked in the smokehouse. The rest of the meat, we canned. Dad also butchered a steer every year, but I don't remember too much about that, except cutting up the meat for canning.

After the lockers came into being, it was much easier. Dad even got so he let them do the butchering. Mom made her own soap from the cracklings. Cracklings are what is left after lard is rendered. Cracklings made good nibbling and a few went into the corn bread. I was so crazy about cornbread, I asked Mom if she couldn't make a cake out of corn meal.

Dad also raised cane to make sorghum. He had a sorghum mill about a half mile from the house. I don't know too much about sorghum making as we children weren't allowed in the mill. All I know is the cane was fed into one end of the mill and sorghum came out the other end. Oh, how good it tasted mixed with homemade butter and eaten on homemade bread. Or used to make gingerbread, cookies, and popcorn balls.

Mom also made taffy. She always gave us kids a small amount to pull. It might have looked grey when we were through, but it tasted good.

We kids would pick wild grapes, plums, and red haws. Mom made jelly and butter from these. Wild gooseberries were also picked, canned, and used for pies. Gooseberries were sometimes mixed with elderberries or mulberries for pies. Elderberries and mulberries are quite bland, gooseberries livened them up.

We lived in a six-room house. Four down and two up. We didn't have electricity, but we did have running water. You grabbed a pail, ran out to the well, pumped a pail of water, and ran back in. We carried water for everything---washing, cooking, etc.

The kitchen and dining room were the heart of the house. The kitchen boasted a large range that burned wood. A large wood box sat near the kitchen stove. There was quite an art to building and maintaining a fire to bake breads, pies, and cakes. Especially, an angel food cake. Mom baked her own bread until the last few years of her life. I can still remember the loaves stacked 24 high when she was feeding a large group and needed leftover bread for the week.

One time Dad told Mom he would leave her if she ever brought a loaf of store-bought bread into the house. Dad must have seen an especially tempting loaf in the store once for he brought a loaf home. Mom was really hurt; she took much pride in her ability to bake bread. Nothing was nicer than coming home from school ravenous, stepping into the house, and smelling that bread! Mom would cut a slice, butter it, and hand it to us. Um-m-m! Who would have doubted she was the best mother in the whole world.

A large bucket was kept in the kitchen to catch all the food scraps, peels, etc. for the hogs. It had to be dumped twice a day and washed. Since the hog lot was quite a ways from the house, this chore usually fell to the older girls and boys.

In the center of the dining room stood a large round oak table, stretched out with as many leaves as possible. It could seat sixteen. During the week, the table was covered with an oilcloth. On Sundays, Mom would use a white linen damask cloth. Dad always sat at the head of the table with Mom to his left. I think she sat in that position to be handy to the kitchen. She was forever jumping up refilling dishes or coffee cups. Mom always saucered her coffee, never spilling a drop.

Meals were a happy time, although Dad didn't put up with any shenanigans. We never had less than five for a meal during the week and on weekends who counted. At one time, Mom was fixing nine school lunches. All the married kids that could come came home for the weekend. No one asked if it was okay, they just knew they were welcome.

During the Depression, a married brother or sister and family lived at home until they found a means of livelihood. In winter in a corner of the dining room, there sat a wood burning heater. You know how those wood stoves work, warm on one side, cool on the other.

The downstairs also had a parlor, which was seldom used, but kept in readiness in case someone important like the preacher came unexpectedly. It was a cold room in winter, but in the summer, a cool room to take refuge for a few quiet moments.

Johnson home by the river and near Stuart, IA

Mom's quiet time was egg-gathering time. She never wanted help with this chore, preferring a few moments alone with the chickens, which probably seemed quiet after the house full of kids. Watching the old hens taking a dust bath or gathering her babies around her can be soothing. I always enjoyed it.

The other room downstairs was Mom and Dad's bedroom. It was a mysterious room to me. This was the room where babies were born (and conceived evidently), where one was nursed through an illness, where death visited. It was a room where the lugs of dried fruit, such as raisins, prunes, apricots, and peaches were stored on top of the high chiffonier. High enough to keep small hungry tykes from snitching and where Dad kept his bottle of medicinal tonic hid in the handkerchief drawer. I never knew Dad to take a drink, maybe it was there just in case.

It was a room where a couple of female relatives would disappear for a bit of gossip or woman talk. On Sundays, the bed would be full of napping babies. We were never forbidden to enter their bedroom, except at Christmas time, but I always felt a little different in Mom and Dad's room---a little awed, a little special.

We had an open stairway leading to two upstairs bedrooms. One was called the "girls room" and the other the "boys room."

Each room contained two double beds. When company came, we kids slept crosswise of the bed up to five or six, depending on the size of the children. If all beds were claimed by adults, we slept on the floor. In the fall, after cornhusking, we made new cornhusk mattresses.

Our room had two dressers. I had one drawer to call my own. It held such treasures as empty matchboxes, my doll, and her clothes, any little tidbit of lace or ribbon, and my Valentines. I kept some of them until 1955. When we sold our home in Flint and moved out of state, I regretfully threw them away.

The open stairway furnished many hours of enjoyment for us kids. We slid down the stairs on our rumps. It's a wonder we weren't calloused. Sometimes we'd sneak a quilt and several of us would tumble down together. The banister too, was good for sliding, the only drawback being the part of the newel post that stuck up.

We had a cellar with an outside entrance, where all our fruits and vegetables were kept. In the fall, Dad would buy several bushels of apples and put them in the cellar. When Dad asked in the evening, "Who wants to get a pan of apples?" he always had a volunteer.

There was a front porch where we spent many summer evenings listening to our elders tell stories. Also, listening to the whip-poor-wills and watching the bats flying by, catching insects for their evening meal.

The attic of the house was full of bats. They flew out a hole at the peak of the roof. Once in a while, they would get into our bedroom. One time, my niece Jean and I heard one screeching. We hollered for Mom and ducked under the covers. Mom came on the run with the broom. She found it in our bed at our feet. There was a back porch on the north side of the house. Many hours were spent there preparing vegetables for canning.

We had many forms of entertainment. We enjoyed our big fenced-in yard. We always had a swing and a trapeze hanging in the big oak tree. We played hide-and-go-seek, Eenie-Annie-Over, jump rope, jacks, drop the handkerchief, and many more. When Mom had time, she played with us. We girls played house with our dolls. We made mud cakes and decorated them with weed seeds. Mom would give us any wormy flour she might have and then we'd raid the sparrow nest for eggs to make noodles. Really, they didn't taste bad. In winter, we played Fox and Geese, Statues, skating, sliding, fort building, and of course, the snowball fights. We also had the timber and the river to roam.

A child was taught to "help out" as soon as he was old enough. Gathering corncobs for kindling was one of the first chores I remember. These we picked up from the hog lot if there weren't any freshly shelled ones at the corncrib. We carried in all the wood for the cook stove and heater, digging it out of the snow in winter.

W.T. Johnson with axe

It seemed we were forever doing dishes. By the time I was born, Mom had a washing machine with a gasoline motor. We carried the water to the washhouse and heated it in a big iron kettle. Mom boiled her white clothes to keep them bright white. We hung the washed clothes on three long lines until the lines were full, and then the overalls were hung on the fence. When it came time to empty the sudsy wash water, it was used to scrub the porches and the privy. One didn't waste water unless you had a strong arm. Another daily chore was filling the lamps with kerosene and washing the chimneys.

The holidays at our house were fantastic. At Christmas, my favorite, Dad brought in a cedar or pine tree that reached to the ceiling. We kids made all the usual decorations using gum wrapper foil and colored paper. We strung popcorn and sometimes we'd have cranberries to string. Mom made a big batch of fudge, sea foam, nougat, popcorn balls, and cookies.

Our gifts were usually homemade or very reasonably priced. People would call them cheap today, but to us they were heaven sent. One Christmas we had 60 brothers, sisters, nieces, nephews, aunts, uncles, and cousins for dinner. Now that's a neat trick to serve so many in two rooms. It did happen to be a beautiful, sunny, warm, 70' outside. So if people felt cramped, they could step outside. Dad always wanted to rent the trustee farm in Des Moines with all its small homes and move the whole family there. Now wouldn't that have been a clan!

Memorial Day we always visited the cemeteries, taking what flowers were in bloom to decorate the graves of loved ones. Iris, peonies, and the old-fashioned yellow roses were usually in bloom. If the cemetery was quite a few miles away, we took a picnic lunch.

May 1st wasn't a holiday, but was a fun day for us kids. We made May baskets, using oatmeal, cornmeal, or any other small box. The boxes were decorated with crepe paper or wallpaper, and then filled with popcorn, homemade candy, and wild flowers. The wild violets were in bloom by then. In the evening, just at dusk, we would start out to hang our baskets on friends' doors. We would sneak up, hang the basket on the door knob, knock, and run. The point being not to let them catch you, or know who you were. They would catch us and join us for the next hanging. We would go all the way around the country block.

On the Fourth of July, we always had homemade ice cream. Dad would go to town and buy the ice. Lucky was the kid that got to lick the dasher.

Easter we hid our eggs. They were always colored the next day. How could the Easter Bunny have found such clever hiding places? All the kids that could came home for the holidays.

One was introduced to life and death at an early age in those days. The first death I remember was my nephew, Keith. He was my favorite playmate. We were both five years old. He died suddenly from a ruptured appendix. In those days, the dead were brought to the home until the day of the funeral, then taken to the church. I can still see a little girl, me, sitting in a big, black leather chair watching Keith at rest, wondering why he wouldn't get up to play with me. After all, he was just sleeping, I was told. When I was eleven, I served as a pallbearer to the two-year-old little neighbor girl who had drowned in a watering tank. The undertaker told us to straddle the grave. He meant with the casket, but the little girl ahead of me actually tried to straddle the grave. On the way to the cemetery, we four young girls had to hold the casket in our laps. Those types of things don't make for pleasant memories.

When I was seventeen, I was with my sister, Dortha, when her second child was born. Dortha was in Mom and Dad's bedroom with Dr. Crews. Mom and Dortha's husband, Frog, were helping. I was in the dining room praying Frog would faint so I could help. And sure enough, he staggered out white as a sheet and I was called in to help. Charlene was a beautiful baby and grew up to be a beautiful girl.

Aunts and uncles came to spend days with us. There was Aunt Sade and Uncle Howard. Uncle Howard's name was really Beauregard Howard. But I didn't know it for years. I think Uncle Bo would have fit him very well. Aunt Sade was Dad's sister. I mostly remember how very, very clean and how very, very strict she was. Uncle Bob, Mom's brother and his wife, Aunt Matt, short for Martha, were so much fun. Uncle Bob would get Dad's old cowhide coat, put it over his head, go outside, and scratch at the windows. It would scare us half to death. We just knew it was a bear and always hid under the table. Mom enjoyed Aunt Matt's company. They were always up to something. One Halloween, Mom and Aunt Matt went out to do mischief. They wouldn't take us kids. Both were in their late 50s, but that didn't stop them. They walked about four miles, soaping windows, sliding down haystacks, and having fun.

Aunt Minnie, Mom's sister, and her gambler husband, Uncle Arthur, came once a year. Aunt Minnie always wore the latest styles and lots of jewelry. Aunt Maud, Mom's sister, and Uncle Tink, Mom's brother also came for visits. Uncle Tink had a large knot on his head that he supposedly got from being conked over the head with a billy club so many times. It was rumored he was a bootlegger. Mom had many more brothers and sisters that I never met. Dad had only one sister and a half-brother. Dad and Mom raised the half-brother, Uncle Otis. We loved them all and looked forward to their visits.

At one time, Mom and Dad took turns having neighborhood dances. All the furniture was removed from the parlor and dining room and the floors waxed. I imagine some local talent played for the round and square dances. I was only about 8 at the time, so after a couple of dances with another young friend, we were sent upstairs to play.

Another thing I remember about Mom---she loved arguing and would argue any side just for the sake of a good debate. She was a feisty one! Mom wrote poetry and had some set to music during the 40s. She loved music. She hated the song *I'll String Along with You*. No one dared sing that song in Mom's presence.

You may not be an angel
Cause angels are so few
But until the day that one comes along
I'll string along with you.

Mom wrote songs and even had some published along with the
music that were made into records.

The other buildings on the farm were many and for varied uses. The washhouse where we did the wash was heated every Saturday evening for baths. That was one of my chores. Every Saturday, I carried water and heated it for the men's bath. In the summer, after working in the fields, they would go to the river for a swim. The smokehouse sat next to the washhouse. The notorious outhouse stood a few feet beyond the yard gate. On a cold, black night with just a lantern to guide you, it seemed a mile away.

Next came the woodpile. The pile never seemed to diminish no matter how much wood we kids carried in. Dad and the boys kept the pile big during breaks in the farming. Dad had a buzz saw to cut the logs into shorter lengths ready for splitting. This saw was very dangerous to use. My oldest sister Ola's husband lost a leg in a sawing accident and bled to death before they could reach him with medical help.

The brooder house sat south of the wood pile. A brooder house is where the baby chicks are cared for until they are ready for the henhouse or ready to be eaten.

The henhouse with its rows of nests and roosts was close by. We usually had 100 layers and a few roosters to keep them happy. Once when I was five years old, I was sent to the barn to call the men for dinner. On my way, a mean old rooster attacked me. I still wear the scar below my left eye. Dad immediately shot the rooster. I must say we enjoyed chicken and noodles the next day.

The garage or tool shed, as it was also called, was the last building before the barn lot. It never housed a car but served as a shop for repair work. It also held fifty-gallon drums full of black walnuts that we gathered in the fall. On rainy days when work was slack, the men would pick out jars of nuts for cookies or caramel popcorn.

Entering the barn lot, there was a feed granary with a hog house attached. The Barn came next. I capitalize "Barn" because it was such an important part of the farm. It housed the horses, the old bull, baby calves, and other animals that needed shelter at the moment.

W. T. Johnson picking corn

Dad had a dairy herd of 35 milkers when I was young. All the cows were milked by hand. I never learned to milk until I was 18, but I did help the boys feed the cows and separate the cream from the milk. We kept tin cups in the barn and when the cow was being stripped, we would catch a cup of warm milk to drink. Delicious!!

The Stuart Creamery came several times a week to pick up the cream. Dad had Holstein cows and a huge mean bull. His pen was especially strong and we children were warned to "steer clear." The men always carried a pitchfork if they were in the pasture with him.

One time our bull got into a fight with the neighbor's bull. Mr. Wagaman was as mean as his bull. When Dad left the house to break up the fight, he took both pitchfork and gun. We never knew but what he would have to use one or the other on the bull or Mr. Wagaman. We were so happy to see him and the bull return unscathed.

Dad raised several head of hogs. One year the hogs came down with cholera. Dad had to destroy all hogs on the farm. He dug a pit, killed all the hogs, and then burned them. He had to wait a certain number of years before he could bring more hogs onto the farm. It must have been heartbreaking.

When the baby animals lost their mother or their mother refused to mother them, Dad brought them to the house for Mom and us kids to start on the road to life. At any one time, a box behind the heating stove held baby pigs, chickens, or lambs.

Evelyn with lamb

We kids played Tarzan in the Barn. Swinging from the rafters and jumping off the rafters into a pile of hay. My brother, Willis, used to catch bull snakes and turn them loose in the barn. Snakes are good mousers. They also love hen's eggs. Reaching into a hen's nest in the barn was very scary. We kids usually preferred to let the hen take her chances on hatching them. When the men would put up hay, Willis and I would collect insects.

Across the road stood a corncrib with three large bins through the center, used to store soybeans, oats, and wheat. We kids weren't allowed to play in the crib. It not only destroyed the grain, but was very dangerous to jump into a bin of wheat, but fun! My niece, Jean, and I loved the corncrib, racing along the narrow boards laid across the corners of the bins. One time, she slipped and fell to the bottom onto about two inches of soybeans. I was sure she was dead, so ran to the house for help. My sister, Dortha, came, but by that time, Jean was up. Of course, Dortha told on us. We felt we'd already learned our lesson. Mom made sure we had, after making sure we weren't hurt.

Dad farmed several hundred acres of rich bottomland. He not only prayed for the right weather, but fought weeds, insects, and the floods. Dad was a respected farmer of the community and his advice was often sought.

The mailbox was half a mile from the house. Our mail was delivered out of Dexter. It was fun to go for the mail. Sometimes there would be our box of Teaberry gum. We'd save cereal box tops and send them in for the gum. What a treat! In the spring and fall, we got the "Sears, Roebuck" and the "Montgomery Ward" catalogs. Our WISH BOOKS. We girls were allowed to cut out the models and clothes for paper dolls from the old catalogs, before they were taken to the outhouse for further use.

We kids attended Pioneer School, 1st through 8th grades. Pioneer was a one-room school. It was an accredited school, which meant that upon graduating from 8th grade, a student could attend any high school in the state of Iowa tuition free. My brothers, Willis, Don, and Clarence, and sisters, Grace and Gladys, graduated from Stuart High School. But I chose Redfield High, so I could live with my married sister Martha who was 12 years older than I. Martha lived only a mile from school and the bus ran past her house.

My junior and senior years, I stayed with the folks and walked one and a half miles to catch the bus. We had a very mean bus driver named Dunbar. "Dennis (Evelyn's son), I too was kicked off the bus one night for fighting with the driver's daughter." He not only kicked me off, but three of my friends, too. He wouldn't let us ride again until our parents talked with him. I still think I was right.

Evelyn 1939

I attended the Union Chapel Church. It was very interesting since it was non-denominational. Everyone had their own views and voiced them. I taught Sunday school to the little ones, believe it or not. The church has been torn down and only a small plaque marks the spot.

Most of the grocery shopping was done by Mom and Dad in the small town of Redfield, Dexter, or Stuart. We children seldom got to go. Occasionally, Mom would bring home a small sack of candy for us. We always divided it up and one seldom got more than two pieces. Those chocolate drops were mighty good.

I went to my first show in Redfield at the age of twelve. We saw *Dracula*. It rained while we were at the theater, so we had a long walk 1 ½ miles home in the mud and dark. Having Dracula follow you home wasn't pleasant.

Once a year, Old Settlers came to Redfield. Oh, what fun! We were given a quarter to spend. What to spend it on was the big decision. The Merry-Go-Round was five cents, the Ferris wheel cost ten cents, and an ice cream cone was five cents. Of course, there were the sideshows, which we weren't allowed to attend.

I was sixteen when I was allowed to attend the dances in Stuart. Oh, they were such fun! At that age, I would rather dance than eat. Even today, I wouldn't mind trying a step or two. Willis and I would put a record on the phonograph and practice our steps. We thought we were pretty good. *Sentimental Journey* was our favorite piece of music to dance to. We practiced our entrance onto the dance floor, our dips, etc.

One night we were doing especially well, or so we thought, dipping and swirling across the dance floor when during a dip, Willis dropped me. There I lay flat on my back in the center of the dance floor, in front of God and everybody. After a good laugh, we continued. The dance of the day was the "Jitterbug." We also round danced, square danced, and did the polka. I remember once when Dad read the book, *From the Ballroom to Hell,* and he forbid me to go dancing for several weeks. Finally, Mom intervened and I was allowed back on the dance floor. I got to read the book a few years later.

Then I met your Dad at a Saturday night dance in Stuart in January, 1946. He was tall and handsome and gee, he could really dance. We were married April 21, 1946 in Boone, Iowa and began our new life in the one room home Joe had built on land across from where his parents lived. And so our life began together!

H. Evelyn Dew's Photographs

Evelyn in sailor suit

Evelyn at home in Stuart

Evelyn and Elaine at Iowa State

Fishing in Canada

Evelyn and Elaine

Evelyn loved Christmas

Evelyn and Dennis 1968

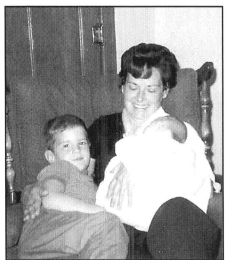

With grandsons Jeff and Brian

Joe and Evelyn's 25th

25th Wedding Anniversary

I. Evelyn Dew's Writings

Raking fields of new mown hay
Gathering eggs that old hens lay
Chopping wood, milking cows
Carrying corn to ten big sows
Planting beans, plowing corn
Five black sheep needing shorn
A farmer's chores are never done
Peace and quiet are seldom won.

Peace and quiet on the old farmstead,
The farmer dreams on his feather bed.

Saturday night and the work's all done
Now to town for a bit of fun.

My Dream

Just a little ray of sunshine,
And a little gurgling laugh,
Just a darling baby, mine,
    That's my dream.

One sweet mass of golden curls,
One cute little dimpled chin,
All enfolded in sky blue furls,
    That's my dream.

He would bring me so much joy,
Oh, how wonderful it would seem,
If God could grant me, a little boy,
    That's my dream.

How I'd love to sing at twilight,
So he'd rest in slumber sweet.
Just to hold him in my arms, one night,
  That's my dream.

What is sweeter, more sublime,
Sleeping in the moonlight's gleam,
Than a darling infant, mine.
  That's my dream.

A home, to me, is not complete,
Unless a dear child's voice I hear,
The little scamper of tiny feet,
  That's my dream.

How I'd love to sit and sew for him,
Pink satins, blue silks, all agleam,
Oh! How sweet he'd look within them,
  That's my dream.

A baby's arms twined 'round me,
The touch of his tiny hand on mine,
Oh, what a wish could be,
  That's my dream.

What a Little Woman Can Do

What a little woman can co,
Make a little butter,
Bake a little bread,
Cook a little pudding,
Dress a lady's head,
Darn a little stocking,
Write a little prose,
Hem a little handkerchief
To wipe a little nose.

The Long Journey by Evelyn Dew 1986

Long ago, three wise men were blinded by a terrible accident. They heard of a wise man who might help them and so decided to make the difficult journey to see him. Gathering a few belongings, the three started out.

The way was arduous. The sun shone unmercifully. Stones caused them to stumble. Hours passed. "We cannot go on," complained the first, "It is impossible. We will never make it." Bent and beaten, one of the wise men turned his back on his friends and returned to the village to sit each day in his chair by the window through which he could not see.

Undaunted, the remaining two continued on their journey. After a time, they came to a fork in the road. "Which way shall we go?" cried the second. "We shall become lost. It is too dangerous." In his confusion and fear, he dejectedly turned back, returning to the village to sit each day in his chair by the window through which he could not see.

Tired and discouraged, the solitary blind man sat down by the side of the road. After a long while thinking in the hot sun, he stood and faced the fork. Just as he was about to step forward, he heard a low voice. "Where are you going?" the stranger inquired.

"I have heard wonderful tales of a wise man who might help me," the blind man replied.

"Here, take my arm. It is on my way." And together, the two continued.

Days passed, but finally the stranger left the blind man at the path to the home of the wise man. The difficult journey was almost at an end. A knock and the old, bearded man appeared. "How may I help you, my son?"

"I have traveled far. I have come for your help and counsel."

"Life is full of long and difficult journeys, my son. You have just completed one. I cannot change your blindness. However, you have already learned the lessons necessary to succeed. To begin, set a goal and pursue it. Do not be dissuaded by those who say it cannot be done, nor stopped by the obstacles in your way. Be willing to trust and accept help along the way. Success will be yours if you persevere and take the journey step by step."

Happiness by Evelyn Dew

The man crawled further up on the sand, gagging on the salty seawater. He was lost in the darkness of the night and the pounding storm.

When dawn broke, his senses slowly returned. He dragged his aching body to an upright position. Before him lay the endless, blue ocean; behind him, a forbidding, green, island forest. The sun was beginning to grow hot. His head throbbed. What was he to do? Was he to be stranded here, alone forever?

Day after day passed and he only just survived. Then he heard the song of an exquisite bird and caught a glimpse of its white body and long tail as it flew deeper into the heavy foliage. At first, he only searched for the bird and tried to hear its melodious call. As time passed, however, he fell under the spell of its song and decided to catch it.

All day long, he was on his quest to capture the white-plumed bird. For weeks, he chased the bird, trying to grab it when it landed on a branch. The companionship he sought flew quickly away.

The bird became very frightened and leery of this strange new creature that was now living on its island. It became more and more elusive until the day came that the man could no longer catch even a glimpse of the white-plumed bird nor hear its song the entire day.

After several weeks of this fruitless search, the man gave up all hope of ever seeing the white-plumed bird again. He began to turn his thoughts to more pressing concerns. He built a shelter and began devising methods for obtaining better food supplies from the sea.

Gratefully, his days filled and he no longer thought of the elusive bird. He began to feel hale and hearty in mind and body. Then one morning, he awoke to the melodious song.

When he came out of his shelter, he frightened the white-plumed bird away, but he did not pursue it, and went about his daily activities. The bird returned and slowly became accustomed to the man's presence. It no longer flew off in fright.

Little by little, the white-plumed bird lost its trepidation. It came closer and closer and stayed longer and longer. No longer did the man have to chase frantically through the underbrush to try to catch a glimpse of it and hear it haunting song.

For the first time since his calamitous arrival on the island, the man felt true contentment. He had learned that the more he pursued happiness, the more it eluded him. It was when he least expected it that it perched outside his window and filled his soul with joy.

J. Miscellaneous Photographs

Ola Johnson (Thompson)'s daughter and granddaughter

Darlene Thompson (McLuen) and Carla McLuen (Hillgren)

Clarence Johnston's daughter Kathy and her husband

Kathy and Chris Lehr

Willis Johnston, wife, and daughter Gwen Day's family

Maxine, Willis Johnston and Derrin, Gwen,Michele, Dennis Day

Willis Johnston's son

Marlin Johnston

Echo (Dew), husband Lee Custer, and children in Boise, Idaho

Echo (Dew) Custer's children

Joe 16, Gene 22, Lana 8, Joanne 15, Larry 10

John Dew and his family

John, Edith, and daughter Mary Dew

John Dew's son

Harold *Leroy* Dew "Curley"

Leroy Dew and his children

LaVon (Asher), Robin (Love), Harold Leroy Dew, Donald, Michael

Arlene Dew Pruett's son

Jack Pruett

Jim Dew's family

Joe, Elaine, Evelyn   Goldie, Jim's wife Dorla, and 4 sons
Dennis

DeElda Dew Kitterman's son and his daughter

Dr. John Kitterman   Julie Kitterman

Joe's classmate Hazel Whitney and her brother

Hazel Whitney
1937

Arnold and Hazel Whitney
2008

Elaine and Larry Briggs

92912854R00164

Made in the USA
Lexington, KY
10 July 2018